THE BIRDS, THE BEES & THE BIBLE
HOW TO PRACTICALLY PARENT SEXUALITY

ZALEA DOLD

ZALEA DOLD

Edited by Nicole Bouwer

Cover design by Annamart van Graan (Dednam Creative)

Formatting by Polgarus Studio

To my girls Chloé-Mari and Zya-Ann

I believe God's Word can change the world, and I
believe that change starts in one's own home.

My most urgent prayer is for God's Word to get to
those who hurt. My second most urgent prayer
is that you, my girls, will take it to them.

I Love You!

Mommy

ACKNOWLEDGMENTS

I am exceedingly grateful for the following people who knowingly and unknowingly assisted me in making this book a reality:

Dr. Darleen Edwards-Meyer: A personal friend, mentor, and one of the best teachers I have ever met. The day you presented your sexuality workshop at the Bible College in 2002, I realized what God was calling me to do. He has used you in many ways to establish in me what was needed to be able to do it. I learned most of what I know about sexuality education from you and Carl, and I want to honor you and your obedience to our Father. Thank you for being part of my life and, of course, for the permission to share some of your wisdom in my book. This 'thank you' also includes the whole team of facilitators in Cape Town—Estelle, Althea, and Carine. I learned so much through working with all of you. Thank you for your input, influence, and friendship.

Frank & Nicole Bouwer: Frank (pastor [B.Th.] and founder of Common Ground Ministries), thank you for checking all my biblical references and thank you for sacrificing time with your beautiful wife to assist me in the editing process. Nicole, working with you was not just an honor, but I also gained a valuable friend for life. You guys are just amazing!

Rika, my parenting expert friend: A casual comment from you sparked the idea of this book, "Stop complaining that you can't speak Dutch; write a book and get your message out that way." It was the nudge I needed. Thank you.

My husband, Ray: Thank you for loving me, even when I fed you leftovers for months on end so that I could finish this book. I love you.

Jesus: The day I met You in November 2001, I knew You were the answer. Not everyone wants to hear it, but I will never stop trying to tell them exactly that!

CONTENTS

PART 3: DON'T STOP NOW! (AGES 12–18+)

A NOTE TO PARENTS

I am so happy that you chose to read my book! It shows that you care deeply about your family's sexuality education. Thank you for the opportunity to share with you what I believe God has placed in my heart.

I wrote this book with an intense passion inside of me. This passion has always been far beyond my understanding. It has been with me since my teenage years, and it was amplified significantly when I gave my heart to Jesus at the age of 23. And finally, at the ripe age of 43 years, God said that IT IS TIME—time to put this passion into words!

That means, though, that I might say something in this book that may lead you to label me as either too conservative or too liberal, or you might disagree with me completely. It comes with the territory. I don't presume that my advice and answers are completely correct. But I do hope, at the very least, that my thoughts will empower you, the parent, to think the matter through and present a better answer to your child as the Lord guides your thinking.

I have also tried not to present certain controversial topics too early (when children are too young), but your child may be confronted with complicated and confusing issues at a much earlier age than you expect. In such cases, I urge you to use or adapt the applicable concepts I discuss in *Part 3* with wisdom and discernment.

I understand that in many homes, the family dynamics are different due to divorce, death or other circumstances. I try to be sensitive to families that don't fit the mold. Unfortunately, I can't anticipate or respond to all the unique needs of families. So please use this book creatively and with discernment to meet the needs of your situation.

I pray that this book will be a valuable tool for you and your family!

Calea

Begin with the end in mind.

— Stephen Covey, *The 7 Habits of Highly Effective People*

PART 1

WHAT TO KNOW BEFORE YOU START

Chapter 1

What to Know Before You Start—The Facts

I will make you my wife forever, showing you righteousness and justice, unfailing love and compassion. I will be faithful to you and make you mine, and you will finally know me as the Lord. **Hosea 2:19–20 (NLT)**

This is my very favorite Scripture. It shows a passionate God who loves me with His whole heart, even when I mess up. (God wanted Hosea to fetch his adulterous wife and love her passionately again, just as He will forgive Israel and love them passionately after they went after other gods.) When I read this Scripture for the first time, I knew that this was what I wanted. If my God can love me so passionately, then surely His plan for marriage is to symbolize the same fervent and zealous love that He has for us. He died for us! If that is not the ultimate passion move, then I don't know what is… All great love stories involve someone who sacrifices greatly. Sexuality within marriage is a symbol of the intimate covenant that He has made with us. It is *so* worth waiting for.

When I eventually got married, this Scripture was engraved into my ring—to remind me of a loving, passionate, righteous God who will never let me go, who wants me to love my husband in the same way, and of the great gift He gave all of us to remind us of His passionate love for us: our sexuality. True intimacy ('into-me-you-see') is something we can only find with Him. No spouse can fulfill that need that we all have. I thank God for the way He tries to show us that fact—by giving us our sexuality. And He wants us to teach it to our children.

A little bit about myself

Before I accepted Jesus into my life, I was involved in a five-year sexual relationship with a man I wasn't married to. We were engaged by the time I was 21 years old. When we broke the engagement in 1999, a month before our wedding and right at the time I graduated with my degree in Fine Arts, I was devastated and heartbroken. I developed an eating disorder because of the rejection I experienced. Even after I gave my life to the Lord in 2001, I kept my struggle with bulimia a secret, thinking that I would be able to overcome it by myself. Oh, how wrong I was. I completed my degree in Post-School Education in 2002 and attended Bible College that same year. I continued growing in the Lord throughout that time, but still told no one about my eating disorder. I started working as a high school teacher in the field of Design and Visual Arts and taught in the United Kingdom (UK) for two years. It was in the UK that I was set free from my struggle with bulimia. It was a long and hard journey of healing, but I emerged victorious! The eating disorder was never about weight issues; I was never overweight. The pain of rejection and the fear of not being accepted and not being good enough were the triggers that made me turn to bulimia as a way to manage the pain in my heart. (But perhaps this story is best left for another book!) I settled in Cape Town soon after my return from the UK in 2007, eager to start a new life free from eating disorders, ready to see what God had in store for me.

During my time at Bible College, I met Dr. Darleen Edwards-Meyer, a specialist in the field of sexuality education. She sparked my passion for this subject and I received my training as a facilitator through her mentorship and programs. Her programs are currently running in many schools and institutions throughout South Africa, Namibia, and Botswana.

The day I met Dr. Edwards-Meyer, it triggered something in my spirit and I just knew that God was calling me to be a part of helping young people and parents in the field of sexuality. It instantly activated a drive within me that I cannot put into words—I just had to be part of the team! I sat under her mentorship for many years and received intensive training on how to present her programs to parents, educators, and the youth.

My passion and interest continued growing as I got older, and I kept educating myself, doing self-study, attending seminars, workshops, and teachings. I continued training in sexuality education throughout my teaching career.

I worked as a high school teacher for 17 years, and all the teenagers that went through my hands will testify that this teacher struggled to stick to her appointed subject. Big parts of my lesson time were spent speaking about sexuality. Sometimes the students would even ask me to stop teaching my subject because they would rather talk about matters related to their sexuality for the rest of the lesson. They had so many questions! They asked about how they can live with their sexual feelings, the 'first time', relationships, marriage, pregnancy, drugs, clubs, parties, pornography and much more. They asked questions they couldn't ask their parents: "How does the body work? How is it even possible to wait for marriage? What does God say? Is there a God?" They wanted to know about spirituality, religion, birth, sexual behaviors, sexually transmitted diseases, sexual choices, and the reasons for all the rules and boundaries. Some even spoke openly about their sexual encounters, heartbreaks, rejection, shame, and fears. I tried very hard to convince them to make good and healthy sexual choices. I preached, I warned, I taught, I cried, I loved, and cared; I role modelled, and I messed up, too. I had countless one-on-one conversations and we had big group discussions. I was transparent about my own mistakes and I did all I could think of doing to show them the way, to change their thinking, and to convince them of the truth of what I was saying.

To this very day, I have no idea if I made an impact on any of them, but I did learn six particularly important lessons.

Lesson 1: A game plan update is necessary.
My own girls will be teenagers one day. If they are going to be exposed to what these kids were exposed to, I must up my game plan as a parent.

Lesson 2: Sexuality education must come from home.
As a parent, you have the most important job in this area of your children's lives. No school can replace your role. Teachers all over the world are doing their best to provide the education, manners, love, and respect that children don't get at home, but if it's not coming from home, those teachers can only do so much. Don't make it their responsibility—it's yours. You are your children's biggest influence in all areas of life, especially in how they view their sexuality.

Lesson 3: Religion doesn't change sexual behavior; relationship does.
You would think that putting your child in a Christian school where they have good ideas, promote good deeds, have good intentions, and make good rules would do the trick. However, after teaching at a Christian school for many years, I noticed that all those things don't change the heart. If a personal relationship with Jesus isn't cultivated at home, the institution can't do much. And that goes for Sunday School as well. I realized that young people are starved for conversation with adults they can trust. They need to feel comfortable to talk about their sexuality, and to be comfortable, trust is needed. And to trust, a relationship is needed.

Lesson 4: Parents need and want help.
I realized that most parents have no idea how to tackle the topic of sexuality with their children, and the children in my class were looking for answers. In

fact, the parents were looking for answers as well! Some students even stayed behind in class during their breaks so that they could chat about all these matters. I sometimes wonder how I ever got through my curriculum in time for the exams. Seventeen years of teaching taught me that those know-it-all teenagers desperately need their parents to show them the way, and that they *do*, actually, need clear boundaries. Teenagers are hungry for answers and if you're not going to teach them who God is—and what He says about sex— the world will teach them everything He is *not*, along with lies about what healthy sexuality is.

I realized that there are numerous reasons why parents don't talk to their children about sex. Some of these reasons are that they might not know how to talk about it, they feel uncomfortable, they fear that the child might perceive it as 'permission' to have sex, they fear that it might damage the innocence of the child, and they fear that the child might have questions about the parents' own sexual experiences. Maybe some parents think that these discussions with their children are overrated because kids know it all anyway. Another possibility is that they might think the children are too young. These reasons are all understandable, but we can't let that stop us anymore. Parenting from a place of fear, ignorance, naivety, or a lack of knowledge is not the way to go. Parenting everything else but ignoring natural sexuality is a recipe for disaster. To be silent about sex sends the wrong message.

Lesson 5: I learned what sexuality education really should be.
Sexuality education is a deliberate process that starts at birth and doesn't end at puberty. In fact, it carries on! It should be filled with intentional discussions between parent and child. It should be a holistic approach that focuses on values and character building and is based on the Word of God while also including information and facts. Sexuality education is not a once- off talk. To only offer information, based *solely* on facts, is incomplete. It ignores values and relationship. It leaves too many gaps that children then fill with unreliable information from other sources: social media and their friends. And we all know what the trend is there!

"But above all else, sex education is about shaping a child's character. Giving the child information is part of that, but only a part. We must also shape the values and attitudes of our kids, shape their worldviews, provide them with the emotional strength they will need to make godly decisions, and instill in them the skills to implement the good decisions they make. Most important, their behavior will spring from their hearts, which will be formed by their personal relationships with and devotion to God. Therefore, influencing their spiritual growth must be a top priority" (Jones and Jones, *How and When to Tell Your Kids About Sex*[29]).

"Education is not the learning of facts, but the training of minds to think." – Albert Einstein

"Educating the mind without educating the heart is no education at all." – Aristotle

Lesson 6: How we talk about sexuality has a massive impact on our children.

There is a right way and there is a wrong way to get God's ideas across to hormonal teenagers. Over-spiritualizing everything, flapping five Bible translations under their noses, pointing out twenty different Scriptures for every statistic you mention, glaring at them over your black-rimmed glasses, dooming them to hell if they mess up, and making statements that induce fear, shame, and guilt are all tactics that won't work. (Believe me, I've tried them all… not the glasses, though.) You can be sure that you will either be creating a rebel who will go out to prove you wrong, or a psychologically messed-up teen with two suitcases full of baggage—or both! That's not what you want. I have worked with such cases, and it's not pretty. I still remember the words of one teacher on the dancefloor at a school function—just as the music switched to a slow-dance tune, she shouted, "LEAVE ROOM FOR THE HOLY SPIRIT," while gently trying to push the couples further away from one another. I don't know about you, but that's not the type of person I would seek out to discuss sexual issues.

Talking only about all the things that can go wrong or scaring them with pictures of sexually transmitted diseases and pregnant fifteen-year-old girls is not going to achieve the desired results. Going with them to the clinic to get birth control pills or buying them condoms is also, to say the least, not exemplary.

A few years ago, when I was teaching at a school, I was called to the principal's office. The mother of one of the girls in my class was complaining about my opinion of her daughter's sexual behavior. "They are using contraception, you know," she said. "And in this day and age, they're all going to have sex in any case." Mother and daughter both felt offended. I felt so sad. This mother was teaching her daughter a lie that she herself believed, the lie that ALL young people have sex and the expectation that young people don't have the ability to control themselves. My heart started aching that day for our youth and also for their parents. A deep urgency was awakened in me to educate not only kids, but the parents as well. Parents need to understand that, as main caregivers and main moral compass shapers, they have the biggest role to play when it comes to their children's sexuality. Sexuality needs to be 'parented'. To this point, my focus had been on the youth only. I realized that the impact on the youth would be much more effective if parents knew how to parent sexuality effectively. Perhaps my approach was wrong or judgmental; maybe I lacked compassion or kindness. Maybe that mom had all the right to be upset with me, but I am thankful for that experience. It made me realize that parents need help, and that how we speak and what we say paves the way for what we want to instill in our young ones. My approach had to change, not my message.

A mother once brought her fifteen-year-old daughter to my husband's chiropractic practice with complaints of neck pain. The girl was a bit uncomfortable at first, but after some elbow-prompting by her trying-hard-to-be-my-daughter's-best-friend mom, she admitted that the neck pain occurred every time she gave her boyfriend a blowjob. It is expected of professional doctors to hide their facial expressions and also, as in this case, withhold their moral opinion. So, although my husband was flustered (to put it lightly), he just treated her and advised her to try to keep her head at a 90°

angle. Back at home, however, he described his experience with a bit more… emotion, and some very interesting facial expressions.

Isn't it heartbreaking that our professions—or the rules of conduct, or 'human rights'—are sometimes stopping us from speaking up and voicing our concerns because we might offend someone? I know there is a time and place for everything, but somehow these excuses became our comfort zone and reason to not speak up for the truth.

How should we approach this subject then?

A better approach for a parent who wants to instill Godly principles and values would be the following:

- Have a non-judgmental approach, especially when you voice your opinion about other people's sexual behaviors.
- Start mastering your poker face and work on the tone of your voice when talking about sexual matters. It should be no different to talking about anything else.
- Be a good listener.
- Always be willing to discuss anything, sharing the truth as age-appropriately as possible.
- Have Scriptures ready for backup and teach them what God says, but don't have a holier-than-thou attitude.
- Don't overreact.
- Be open and honest about your own life (in an age-appropriate way).
- Most of all, always bring whatever question they have back to God's original plan.

Do this with love, positivity, examples, experience, and scientific, biblical facts. Never talk to them about these issues in a condemning or condescending way. Be kind and don't beat around the bush.

In other words...

First, I would like to ask you a few questions: What did your parents tell you about sex? Would you have wanted it to be different? What did social media tell you about sex? Was it accurate and truthful? Whose voice was the most influential in your life when it comes to sex? And when it concerns your own children, do you want to do it better?

Part of parenting our children is to parent their sexuality as well and to place it where it belongs. Your values, beliefs, attitudes, and behaviors about sex will be burned into your children's hearts and minds forever. If you don't parent their sexuality, you are leaving it to the world to impart its 'wisdom', and it will definitely not be in line with what a loving God wants to teach your little prince or princess about His gift of sexuality!

God made us to be sexual beings, as a part of all the other things we are. He wants us to take joyful satisfaction in the pleasures of sex. That is why He tells us what sex really means and how to experience it in a way that honors Him, our spouses, and ourselves. He made us to be sexual beings so that we can know a supernatural and extraordinary unity with our spouses. Yes, it is a physical act, but it has so much emotional and spiritual significance. Sex joins a man and a woman into one flesh, creating a physical, emotional, and spiritual bond between them. If you doubt the emotional and spiritual elements, take an objective look at the people you know who treat sex as a form of casual recreation. Do they exhibit joyful satisfaction with their lives? Do they appear at peace with themselves? Do you think that they are really having as much fun as they claim they are? How are their relationships with other people?

So rather have a vision, clear direction, and a proactive plan of action to effectively parent your children in this area of their lives throughout all the phases of growing up. This is especially important in today's heavily sexualized world. You cannot afford to just hope for the best.

On the day of my daughter's 9th birthday, a boy in her class wanted to show her pornographic images on the school's computer. Even though I was completely freaked out by the fact that information of that nature was accessible on the school's system, I was more worried about the fact that it was an eight-year-old boy who had wanted to show her those pictures! What made me feel a whole lot better was that my daughter was prepared. Because of our previous discussions about this topic, she knew that she shouldn't look, and she knew how to handle it. She told him, "No, I'm not allowed to look at pictures of sex." Then she told me about it, without any fear at all of what my reaction would be. I was so proud of her—not because she didn't look at the pictures, but because she told me about it. Following this incident, we had another great talk about sex, the Internet, God's special gift, and why we should protect it. She might not always look the other way in the future, but at least she knows that if she does look, she can tell me about it. And we can work through it together.

So, while you are still the hero in their eyes, while they are still little, while they still believe everything you say, you have to start teaching them the truth and you have to be the first one to give them the right information. The ideal is to do this before puberty takes over and they see you as the world's biggest, most old-fashioned embarrassment currently alive on earth. Everything that they will experience and learn will be compared to and judged by what *you* taught them. If we compare the brain to a computer, we can say that it's your job to open that file first!

God wants families. Healthy, happy families are the backbone of a healthy society. Families, marriage, sex… it was all His idea (Genesis 1:26–28; 2:24). It might look a bit different in different cultures, but God had a plan, and that plan hasn't changed. People, culture, education, and times have changed, but God's original plan remains the same. If we stick to God's plan, there will be no issues. If we don't, well, we will have to deal with the consequences, and we just have to look around us to see what happens when we deviate from God's Word. If we understand, accept, and live God's intent for our sexuality, it will be much easier to guide our children in this area.

So, what must we do?

1. Wake up

It's time to wake up. The gift of sexuality is under serious attack—in our homes, in the workplace, in schools and universities—everywhere. Do you seriously think a few random chats about sex is going to cut it?

John Maxwell said, "People say there are two kinds of learning: experience, which is gained from your own mistakes, and wisdom, which is learned from the mistakes of others."

We also learn by seeing, hearing, feeling, touching, copying, speaking, trying, falling, and repeating. Through practice and repetition, we improve, like an artist or a sportsperson. The more they repeat it, the more it becomes a habit, and then it becomes part of their lifestyle. If all these steps are necessary for us to learn something well enough for it to become a lifestyle, how can we just leave godly morals and values in our children up to chance or up to others? Can we only rely on having a once-off talk with them or just a few attempts?

If you want your children to have godly values, morals, and principles, you need to up your game and make sure you address it every day. You need to have a goal, clear direction, and a plan of action to implement, and make sure that you deliberately 'practice' every day. Talk to them, listen to wise people's advice, read the Word, and read books. Be consistent, practice, be an example, show them the way, walk in it yourself, speak life, teach truth, pray, and repeat, repeat, repeat... These are all verbs, and it is a daily practice— one that cannot be left to chance or up to others. The enemy wants your children. He wants them badly. And his weapons are not of this world.

How do you fight an invisible enemy? Ephesians 6:12 (NLT) says, "For we are not fighting against flesh-and-blood enemies, but against evil rulers and authorities of the unseen world, against mighty powers in this dark world, and against evil spirits in the heavenly places." If this is the case, why do we still think that we can outwit the devil with a clever theory, a once-off talk about sex, or a few discussions about some facts? Our kids are fighting for their lives, for their souls! Just look around…

According to studies conducted with regard to current sexual behavior:

- A total of 41% of high school students disclosed that they have had sexual intercourse.[2]
- First-time sexual experiences indicated to have been with a steady partner was noted by 73% of teenage girls and 58% of teenage boys.[4]
- First-time sexual experiences indicated to have been with a friend or someone they had just met was noted by 16% of the girls and 28% of the boys.[4]
- Many teenagers reported that they are taking part in sexual activities other than intercourse: about 50% have had oral sex and just more than 10% have had anal sex.[1]
- Drugs or alcohol was used before partaking in sexual intercourse by 21% of teenagers who had had sexual intercourse within the three months before the study was conducted.[2]
- Just more than 11% of the teenagers reported that they have had four or more sexual partners.[2]
- A total of 3.9% of the high school students reported having had sexual intercourse for the first time before the age of 13 years.[2]
- Of the high school students, 10% disclosed that they have experienced dating violence i.e. being kissed, touched, or physically forced to have sexual intercourse when they did not want to, by someone they were dating or someone who they went out with one or more times.[5]

- In total, 7% of high school students reported having been physically forced to have sexual intercourse when they did not want to.[5]
- Women aged 15–19 years is the group with the highest rate of unintended pregnancies of all the age groups.[3,10]
- Females' likelihood of using contraception reduced by 20% with every additional partner they have had.[6]
- Nearly 20 million new sexually transmitted infections (STIs) are reported annually in the United States.[11]
- Young people (ages 15–24 years) account for 50% of all new STIs, although they represent just 25% of the sexually experienced population.[4]
- Both young men and young women are heavily affected by STIs, but young women face the most serious long-term health consequences. Estimations are that undiagnosed STIs cause about 24,000 women to become infertile annually.[11]
- Compared to older adults, sexually active adolescents aged 15–19 years and young adults aged 20–24 years of age are at higher risk for acquiring STIs, because of a combination of behavioral, biological, and cultural reasons.[4]
- Statistics about Pornhub, a popular pornographic website, showed that in 2019 there were 42 billion visits to the website (which equates to 115 million views a day), 39 billion searches performed, 6.83 million videos uploaded, and 1.36 million hours of new content added (which would take 169 years to watch). This means that if you started watching in the year 1850, you would still be busy watching today. There are over 219 985 video views per minute every minute on Pornhub.[7]
- Pornhub is the sixth most visited website in the world, ranking just beneath Google, YouTube, Facebook, Wikipedia, and Twitter— getting even more views than Instagram![7]
- It has been reported that numerous videos of trafficked children have been found on Pornhub, as well as videos of children being raped.[12]

- There has been an explosion of 4,000% in children identifying as transgender: the number of people identifying as transgender is on the rise in the United States and the United Kingdom, including many children and teenagers. Doctors have been accepting cases of underage girls who identify as males and they are performing double mastectomies on these children to avoid the trauma of developing breasts. Some physicians in the United States are performing double mastectomies on healthy girls as young as 13 years old—the justification for this is gender dysphoria or transgenderism—the girls now identify as boys and therefore want to look like boys.[9]
- In England, 800 dysphoric children were injected with puberty-blocking drugs, including some as young as 10 years old.[9]
- Between 2008 and 2018, the rate of teenage girls aged 13–17 years in Sweden being diagnosed with gender dysphoria grew by approximately 1,500%.[9]
- According to a recent survey, half of the US Christians interviewed said that casual sex between unmarried, consenting adults is sometimes or always acceptable.[13]
- All the above (and there is so much more that I am not even mentioning) include Christians.

If these are the facts and this is the world we live in, are we really too lazy, busy, or preoccupied with other things to parent our children's sexuality? Are we too uninvolved, careless, and overworked to fight for them? Come on, people! These are our children! It is our job! You fight this battle on your knees. You fight it by talking, telling, showing, walking, reading, being, teaching, praying, repeating, repeating, and repeating. And when you mess up, fall down, or get tired, you get back up and you do it again. BUT YOU DO NOT LIE DOWN! YOU STAND UP. And if you do not know what to do, you just stand. You are still. And you KNOW who is your God (Psalm 46:10). And then you start again. You are not going to fight a war with a spoon when you have a knife pointing at you. You are going to figure out the enemy's tactics, you are going to learn about his weapons, and you are going to come back with a sword (Ephesians 6:17)!

Be aware, and don't be scared to stand your ground when you experience a temper-tantrum, tween-tantrum or teenage-tantrum with the 'eye roll', the 'door slam', or the backchat. Be aware, and don't be scared to raise issues, talk about uncomfortable things, point out dangers, or to be uncool. Be aware and don't be scared to speak life and truth, and to guide, teach, and show your young ones the way. Be aware and don't be scared to ask for forgiveness, to stand up, and to grow up. Be aware and don't be scared to love, fight, trust, and teach and to *be* the parent. God gave you that authority. Use it wisely. God is your parent, and He did not give up on you.

2. Buckle up

… and by 'buckle up' I mean with God's armor, because sexuality education starts at birth. Before they can even walk, you have already given them hundreds of messages about their sexuality. And it carries on for life.

You must choose to parent their sexuality *intentionally* and *deliberately*. This book is just a guide, but I believe that it can change the way you parent this area, and because this lifelong education comes from *you*, the parent, the outcome can and will be lasting and life-giving for the next generation.

I know you might be thinking that it will take a miracle for you to guide this area of sexuality in your parenting, and you are right. But we also serve a God of miracles, don't we? I truly pray that this book will make you more determined to tackle the area of sexuality in your households head-on.

Know your enemy. But know your God better.

The next generation is worth it.

One day or day one. You decide.

— Paulo Coelho

PART 2

WHERE TO START

(AGES 0–12)

Chapter 2

Know Your Goal—Why Are You Doing This?

Goal 1: A Lifestyle of Purity

You might be thinking, "My child is still small, so why bother with the sexual stuff right now?" The reason is that a *lifestyle of purity* is going to be your goal. It is a lifelong process of teaching and modeling by you—the parent—and it starts when they are born. If you have a goal in mind, you have direction and intention. You will be more focused and deliberate in your mission. You know what you are aiming for and you will not get lost along the way. A goal keeps us on track. Zig Ziglar once said, "If you aim at nothing, you will hit it every time."

Goal 2: Preparation

Our children need to be prepared. The reason for this is that children are targeted in the area of sexuality at a much younger age than previous generations were, with greater intensity, and with much less mercy. They need skills, wisdom, tenacity, resilience, determination, strong character and, above all, the Holy Spirit. Otherwise, goal one won't be attainable.

Let's dissect purity

To be pure is to not be tainted, to be holy, to be free of dirt, and to be spotless and clean. Basically, we all fall short—no surprises there! Purity addresses all areas of our lives: How we dress, how we speak, what we say, what we listen to, and what and who we surround ourselves with.

Purity is not the same as abstinence. Abstinence is the choice to abstain from sex before marriage; it is an action. Purity is a *lifestyle*. If you choose to abstain from sex itself but you still do all the other stuff, does that reflect a lifestyle of purity? If I am a big flirt, I look at pornography, watch sinful movies, or sing along to dubious music, but I am not having sex, am I then living a life of purity? If I dress provocatively to entice a man, am I encouraging him to live a life of purity? If I am dishonest and I gossip, use illegal drugs, get drunk, manipulate people to get my way, lie, or I am disrespectful towards others in the way that I speak to them or act towards them, do I live a life of purity?

A lifestyle of purity is greatly reflected in how we speak. During World War II there was a poster in the United States that read, *"Loose lips sink ships."* It reminded soldiers to be watchful—watchful of what they disclosed when they wrote home and watchful of what they said when they talked to their family and friends when they were on leave. Chance remarks and careless boasts could have revealed military strategy to the enemy, resulting in harm or death to US troops. In the same way, loose lips (flirtatious kidding, suggestive poses, seductive come-ons, gossip, slander, angry outbursts, temper tantrums, biting words, dirty jokes, vulgar and obscene language) may be innocently expressed in 'adult' conversations, but it doesn't stem from a mind that is fixed on Christ. Rather, its origin is a mind that entertains lustful thoughts and worldly values. It shows a spirit unwilling to give up the temporary thrills of worldly conduct for the dignity of godly behavior.

Purity is also reflected in how we dress. God is not asking us to wear head-to-toe robes. We are free to wear what we want to, right? After all, God looks at the heart, right? That is true, but men and women look at each other. Through our choice of clothing, we imply certain messages. A woman who goes out in a skintight dress and low décolletage shouldn't be shocked if she finds herself to be the object of unwanted attention. A man who struts through the office with an unbuttoned shirt and heavy gold jewelry should not wonder why he is not considered for the next available promotion. Immodest attire can easily send the wrong message. God wants our outfits, our speech, and our mannerisms to tell a different story. You are *in* the world, not *of* the world. You must be aware of the signals you send with your appearance, your speech, your mannerisms, and how you treat people, because it reflects who you really are: God's beloved child. It is your sacred privilege to dress accordingly. You can't start talking to your teenage daughter about purity, integrity, dignity, character, or common sense just as she is about to walk out of the house with a skirt that just about covers her vagina. (Those exposed bum-lines are grinning at you, by the way, and camel toes are only pointing one way.) By that time, all grounding should have been done already. I'm not saying that it's too late completely, but your job will be so much harder if you only start when she is 15 years old.

I'm not for one moment suggesting that you should be a prude, dressing only in blue paisley dresses buttoned all the way up to your nose, hair in a tight bun, and allow only gospel music and flesh-toned sports bras in your house. We are sexual beings, and so are our children. We don't suddenly become sexual beings when we get married. However, dressing is a metaphor of who we are and what we want. My mom always said, "Your dresses should be tight enough to show that you're a woman, and loose enough to show that you're a lady." Let's be aware of the signals we send, as purity doesn't just refer to how we behave sexually. God wants holiness in every area of our lives.

Stuff we do to help us 'stay pure'

I'm sure you have heard about the concept of a purity ring or a promise signed on a piece of paper that vows abstinence from sex before marriage. These are great ideas. Nonetheless, it can be just another emotional promise made because all your friends at youth camp were lining up to do the same. I mean, imagine if you decided not to sign that piece of paper! The judgmental looks you would get… But what about the guilt and shame that can follow if you break your purity promise? I am not saying that this concept is nonsense or that you were not sincere when making that promise. Good intentions, however, do not bring us very far. What I am saying, is that it can be a great tool and it definitely has potential to help the cause—if backed up with more than just the 'purity narrative'.

I once heard of a few moms who followed another approach. Each mom took her daughter to buy a bow tie for her future husband, which she then hung in her room as a visual reminder that her husband is a living human being somewhere on earth right at this time, and that she is protecting her purity *for him*. It also serves as a reminder to start praying for that man already. Teenage boys can perhaps buy a tiara as a visual reminder that their future wife is out there somewhere and that they are guarding their purity for their queen.

I believe that this is a wonderful reminder of the whole concept, as it's not just a piece of paper but something more tangible. It can be a great tool if used correctly and if it's accompanied by ongoing discussions about sexuality. Virginity is one of the most precious gifts we can give each other, but we should not raise our kids in a legalistic, religious way in this area. Otherwise, they will grow up with shame and feelings of guilt if they even just have a sexual thought or if they mess up and cross the line. We must teach them what God's intent is for our sexuality, and *why* our sexuality is important to God. It's not just about 'saving sex for marriage'.

We must remember to teach them that when they make the right choices in the area of sexuality, they are guarding themselves *for* something (their future spouse), not just *against* something. One is empowering, the other one is merely obeying a command through resistance. To work towards an end goal is much more motivating than just obeying rules. In any case, rules are meant to be broken, according to teenage 101, so keep that in mind when you are tempted to take that approach. Not one of the teenagers I have ever met or worked with (and I have worked with thousands) will eagerly nod their heads in acceptance when you lay a bunch of dos and don'ts out in front of them.

So how and when do we start teaching our children about purity?

Teaching our children the concept of walking in purity is something that should start at birth. There is no recipe, no 'quick' way, and no set of rules. The Holy Spirit teaches us purity, and without Him our attempts are just empty words, and it borders on dead religion. Be watchful to not be a hypocrite as a parent. If you are not living such a life of purity that your children can see it without you having to say a word, but you want your children to live pure lives, then you are being hypocritical. Behavior to watch out for in your own life is the following: The way you dress, the way you speak, the movies you watch at home, the company you keep, the way you conduct yourself, saying one thing but doing another, dropping them off at church but going back to bed yourself, putting them in a Christian school but not teaching them how to have a relationship with the living God. These are all ways in which your 'walk and talk' might not line up with each another, so be aware of your own behavior.

Keep in mind that this is not an easy task. If you don't make room for mistakes, if you are judgmental and have no love and forgiveness—for yourself and your children—you are going to ruin what can be the best relationship you will ever have. We all make mistakes. Teach them how to repent and go to God. Talk about it. Confess your own mistakes. Show them how it should be done. Living in purity doesn't mean that there are no mistakes. Living in purity means cultivating a lifestyle of mostly good choices and a humble, teachable heart when you do mess up. Unfortunately, parents sometimes create very high expectations for their children. Of course, it is wise to keep the bar set high when it comes to sexual purity, but we live in a sex-crazed world and our children are bombarded with sexual stimulation daily. When we teach them to walk in purity, we also need to teach them how to take mistakes, failures, and sin to God. Fear and shame keep us in our sin, while confession and honesty bring healing. An alarming number of young women, Christians included, are trapped in secret sins such as self-harm, eating disorders, addiction, and sexual sin. The enemy's mission is to cause our children to believe that their actions are beyond God's forgiveness and that if their secret ever came out, their friends and family would be ashamed of them. Girls are particularly good at hiding feelings of shame; thus, it is crucial that you talk to them about this often. Show them how to take such occurrences and feelings to God. Radiate grace and understanding when speaking about the sins of others (without judgement) and confess your own sins with humility and honesty. God will forgive all sins when we confess and repent (John 3:20–21; 1 John 1:9). Children are more likely to seek help if they believe in God's forgiveness and know that you believe in it, too.

Let me give you a simple example of how I handle my mess-ups. In the past, when I lost my temper, I would shout at my kids. The way I spoke to them in those moments of anger was unacceptable, so when I calmed down, I would go to them to apologize for my outburst and ask their forgiveness. I would say, "When I was angry with you earlier, I shouted at you and I was disrespectful in the way that I spoke to you. I should have waited until I calmed down and spoken kindly, because I know I can be kind when I am angry, even if it is hard. I am sorry. Do you forgive me? Can we pray together and tell God what happened? Then I can ask Him to forgive me, too." It's amazing how the hurt in their eyes disappears when I 'man up'. They immediately want to get closer and connect with me again. By apologizing, I restore our relationship and trust, and I teach them how to do it when they mess up themselves. If I just left the situation without revisiting it and repenting about it and I just carried on preaching about forgiveness and being kind, but I myself let rip, I would be sending them mixed signals and not setting the right example. How can I then one day teach them to be kind, honest, open, and respectful to others? How can I one day have 'purity discussions' if I compromise in front of them? To take it even further, how can I teach them to respect the opposite sex if I belittle my husband or wife? How can I forbid my daughter to wear a certain type of shirt if my boobs are out there for all to see? I don't have to be perfect to teach them to walk in purity, but I need to realize that I also need Jesus' forgiveness and grace. Like David, ask God to search your heart, to test you and, if there is any offensive way in you, to lead you on the way everlasting (Psalm 139:23–24).

We cannot...

… make our kids' choices for them (oh, how I wish I could!) and we cannot expect perfection. They are not always going to choose to do the right thing, neither will you and I. We cannot protect our kids from everything or prevent negative things from coming their way.

But here are some things we can do:

- Equip them with tools and strategies and teach them how to use it— your child's needs, lacks, mistakes, and hard circumstances can be counteracted by the tools that God gives us. It will strengthen, arm, and empower them to grow and be victorious. It will help them to make the right decisions and it will put them in a better position to control their emotions and choices.

- Teach by example.

- Choose—every day. Evil does not always look like a snake. It comes in the form of temptation, beauty, lust, gossip, and 'innocent' apps on our smartphones. Satan is a master deceiver. Every day, a few times a day, we need to choose between right and wrong. Teach your children from a young age to recognize the enemy and teach them how to fight it.

- Teach them to hear God's voice.

- Draw on your own experiences. When I speak to teenagers about these matters, it helps to bring in my own experiences because it makes me more real, honest, and human to them. I have found that they relate to me better, open up more, and listen more intently.

A few years ago, a sweet, quiet girl in my class approached me to ask how to deal with the fact that she had sent naked pictures of herself to a guy. If I had been a judgmental perfectionist with a long list of religious rules about sexual purity, she wouldn't have talked to me about it, and I would have lost a great teaching opportunity to impart some wisdom. I also would have lost her if I had overreacted or told her how stupid she was for doing something like that. In answering her question, I used the example of a dear school friend of mine who also sent naked pictures of herself to a guy when she was at university. (If I had done it, I could have used myself as an example.) I told her about the disastrous consequences of my friend's choice, how she had dealt with it and what she had learned from it. I still remember the conclusion the girl came to after the whole ordeal, "I don't want to be someone's sexual fantasy. That's not even real, it doesn't last, and it will be replaced by another fantasy. I want to be someone's love. Every woman on this planet has a vagina and boobs, so me showing my body to whoever is willing to look is not going to make me be more loved. I want to be pursued for who I am, not for what I have. And when he loves me enough to marry me, then I will give him the gift of my sexuality. I would rather have the respect of a man than the lustful eye of one that will always wander." The information she received made this young teenager understand something about the preciousness of her sexuality.

- As the parent, don't just change channels and ignore what appears on television. Rather pause, talk about it, and bring it back to God's original plan for sexual feelings and where those feelings belong. Talk about the outfits, language use, body language, and what it portrays. If you dress to sexually entice, you will attract the man who wants to be enticed. If you behave stupid to attract boys, you will attract stupid boys. It will not be the 'I-want-to-marry-and-love-you-forever' type.

When you have these discussions with your young ones, remember to be gentle, positive, and uplifting, and to portray peace and love. In marriage, sex is safe and free, wonderful and fulfilling, secure and uplifting, fun and exciting. Teach them to be able to know the difference between unbuttoning that extra button or not, having your skirt just a few centimeters longer or shorter, choosing a movie with an age restriction or rather walking away, and spending more time with people who take you away from God or with people who point you towards Him. Are you going to allow the lustful thought to take root and make a nest in your head? Or are you going to choose to stop thinking lustful thoughts and to rather get up and make yourself some coffee? Living in purity of thought flows through to our actions. It is a choice we make every minute of every day in every area of our lives.

If girls and boys can have *lifestyles* of purity, the world will have much less problems in the area of sexuality. It is something that is totally worth pursuing.

But don't think that is enough

Just remember that promise rings, bow ties and purity talks are not enough—not anymore. Maybe, if you live in a cave somewhere, or under a rock, completely cut off from this world, then a once-off discussion about the birds, the bees and the Bible might do the trick in terms of your children's purity. But look around—what is the success rate in church, in our homes, and at schools when it comes to sexual purity? Do you have any idea what your kids are exposed to? I mean, do you *really* know? And what if that which they are exposed to is completely different to what you were exposed to at their age? (Which it is!) Surely then you can understand that today's parents have a very big problem and need a better strategy.

I read two wonderful articles by Juli Slattery, *Promise Rings and Purity Talks Aren't Enough* and *What's the Purpose of Sexuality if I'm Single?* I include both here for you to think about.

<u>*Promise Rings and Purity Talks Aren't Enough,*</u> by Juli Slattery[14]

Christian singles need more than the purity narrative of "save sex for marriage."

"True Love Waits." "I Kissed Dating Goodbye." Promise rings. For the past several decades, the Christian community promoted these touchstones of sexual purity with arguably good intentions. Yet the word purity among today's Christian adults can elicit feelings of shame and even anger.

Why? Because the "purity narrative" has proven to be ineffective for many and harmful for others. If you attended church youth group as a teen, you're probably familiar with the importance of "saving yourself for marriage." You learned that God created sex for marriage and that staying sexually pure is one of the greatest goals of Christian singles (and their parents). Implicit in the narrative is a quasi-promise that if you say no to sex now, someday God will bring a wonderful spouse and you will have incredible, guilt-free sex. If you have messed up sexually, God still loves you and has a plan (though maybe plan B) for your life.

As the mother of teenagers, I understand the importance of emphasizing sexual purity. However, sexuality within our chaotic relational culture is not so cut and dry as "save yourself for marriage, get married and then enjoy great sex." In our efforts to simplify the message, we have failed to communicate the greater vision of God's design for sexuality.

The Purity Narrative Fails

Jenna is one example of the purity narrative failing to teach about God and sexuality. A child of the 90s, Jenna was raised in a godly, loving family and went to church every week. In terms of sexual purity, she's been there and bought the T-shirt (and the promise ring). Now in her late 20s, Jenna's view of sexuality is a hot mess.

Jenna recently broke up with a Christian guy who persuaded her to do everything but have sexual intercourse. She's shackled by guilt because of the lines she has crossed. She's angry at her parents for their narrow views on sexuality and wonders if her whole Christian life has been a sham. All the while, Jenna has friends (Christians and non-Christians) who claim to be reveling in shame-free sex and every form of sexual experimentation. Where is God in the middle of this chaos? Where is the Prince Charming she was promised if she stayed pure? Did she ruin her chances for great sex in marriage by going too far with her boyfriend? Why do her friends seem so much happier than she feels?

The purity narrative, while emphasizing the importance of saving sex for marriage, failed to prepare Jenna and people like her for a biblical approach to sexuality. Here are a few reasons why.

The purity narrative doesn't give context for other sexual struggles.

The power of a narrative is being able to identify your story within the larger story. Many people simply can't find themselves in the story of the purity narrative. What does "save sex for marriage" mean to a Christian who struggles with compulsive masturbation? To a Christian who battles same-sex attraction? How does the purity narrative help if you get married only to find that sex is a major source of conflict? What if you get married and find you or your spouse has no sexual desire?

Honoring God with our sexuality involves so much more than saving sex for marriage. It encompasses how we think and respond to every sexual issue, including how we love people who disagree with a biblical sexual ethic. As the sexual challenges and questions in our day expand, we need a narrative that is large enough to encompass all aspects of our sexuality.

The purity narrative doesn't acknowledge that singles are sexual.

There is far more to our sexuality than what we choose to do with our bodies. Many who grew up with a purity emphasis translated "save sex for marriage" into "it's wrong to be sexual." Christian singles naturally experience sexual physical longings as well as the emotional desire to share life with someone. Those are natural aspects of our sexuality. We don't magically become sexual people because we get married. We choose to steward those desires differently based on marital status.

Simply acknowledging that Christian singles are sexual people brings clarity and relief to those who have been taught otherwise. Our encouragement and teaching on sexuality must go beyond "God created sex for marriage." God also has a purpose for our sexuality as singles.

The purity narrative reinforces the idea that sexual desire is shameful.

A hangover of the purity movement is the assumption that sexual passion is always wrong. I've talked to many Christian married people who have carried this lie into marriage (so many that I can't even tell you the number). Christian women hope for a switch to flip on when they get married. For some, it never seems to activate. Sexual responses are wired into the brain as a sensation or action is linked with an emotional response. The brain can be rewired, yet consistently pairing sexual sensations with feelings of guilt can lead to sex and shame consistently co-existing.

Without realizing it, a person can suppress sexual desire, expression and passion in marriage, afraid of violating God's standard of holiness. The majority of those who have emphasized sexual purity never intended for this outcome, but we can't deny the unintentional fallout.

The purity narrative divides people into categories.

One of the greatest complaints against the purity movement is that it inherently divides people into two categories — those who are sexually pure and those who are not. Those categories easily become the self-righteous saint and the shameful sinner described by Jesus in Luke 18. The determining factor of where you fit is whether or not you are a technical virgin — saving sexual intercourse for marriage. Yet our sexual purity is not so cut and dry.

What about the woman who has done everything except have sex with a guy? And what about using porn, erotica, fantasy or masturbation? Are these people pure or not? And after getting married, what about the husband who uses his wife as an outlet for his lust? Is he pure? Where do those who have been sexually violated fit in? Even though date rape or sexual abuse wasn't their choice, those who have experienced such trauma usually wrestle with feelings of defilement and often act out sexually as a result.

Sexual purity is not as simple as the purity narrative suggests.

The purity narrative is inconsistent with biblical truth.

Think about the overarching message of the Gospel. The fact is none of us is 100 percent sexually pure — we have all missed God's "plan A" of perfection. Our purity, according to Scripture, is determined by the blood of Jesus Christ, not by our sexual choices. There are not some people who need Jesus more than others; as the Bible says, all of us have sinned and are "dirty" before God. It is only Jesus' atoning death on the cross that supernaturally presents us as a pure and spotless bride.

I don't want to diminish the value of purity and sexual integrity. I was blessed to first experience sex on my honeymoon and am grateful for my parents and teachers who encouraged sexual purity. However, I've been humbled by dear friends who didn't grow up like I did … friends who experienced sexual trauma and friends who slept around. The truth is I need the redeeming blood of Christ as much as my friends do. Living as the "pure in heart" is a lifelong challenge in all areas of life, made possible only by the power of the Holy Spirit. And the purity narrative fails to communicate this.

Finding a Biblical Narrative

If the purity narrative is failing, what do we do? Secular culture is aggressively promoting a compelling sexual narrative rooted in humanistic thought. It goes like this: Your sexuality is an important part of your identity and personal expression. To be a mature person, you should explore your sexuality. This is part of becoming who you are as an individual. Anyone who discourages or limits your sexual expression is doing you harm. *As this cultural narrative is gaining momentum, the church does need to respond, but its response needs to be more comprehensive and compelling than "save sex for marriage."*

Sexual integrity is an important element of following Jesus Christ, but it is not so narrowly defined as walking down the aisle as a virgin. In contrast to the purity narrative, the biblical narrative *of sexuality gives us a broader context from which we can understand the bigger picture of why our sexuality matters to God.*

In the biblical narrative, we affirm that God created sexuality as a powerful metaphor to teach us of His covenant love. Every one of us — single or married, male or female, sexually active or celibate — has something to learn about God's love through the experience of our sexuality.

The Bible, from cover to cover, presents a rich explanation of our sexuality, which goes far beyond what many churches have traditionally taught. In the wake of the purity movement, many Christians are giving up on biblical sexuality, choosing instead to embrace a cultural, humanistic view of sexuality. It's time to discover the biblical narrative that can help us make sense of the real challenges we face within the realm of human sexuality.

What's the Purpose of Sexuality if I'm Single? by Juli Slattery[15]

It's not just about sex. Your sexuality has spiritual and relational significance.

For many Christians, the extent of their biblical sex education was the encouragement to "save sex for marriage." While valid that advice has proven to be at best insufficient in light of real-life sexual questions and tensions (read my other article about why the purity narrative isn't enough). What's the purpose of sexuality if I'm single? What if I never get married? In other words, why did God create us as sexual people and why does He care so much about how we steward our sexuality?

Sexuality is confusing to many of us because we do not understand its underlying purpose. By responding to practically every sexual question with some version of "save sex for marriage," we have missed the larger explanation that helps us make sense of biblical sexuality. And that's why this next statement might shock you:

God did not create sexuality primarily *for marriage.*

As a single, the stewardship of your sexuality is not simply to keep yourself pure until God gives you a spouse. Your sexuality has spiritual and relational significance that far surpasses saving sex for marriage.

His Covenant Love

God designed us as sexual people to teach us about something — and marriage is only an echo of it. He intentionally created our sexuality to be a metaphor that teaches us of His covenant love. Every one of us, single or married, male or female, sexually active or celibate, has something to learn about God's love through the experience of our sexuality.

If this is a strange thought to you, consider what John Piper wrote: "The ultimate reason (not the only one) why we are sexual is to make God more deeply knowable."

Think of it this way: Everything God created on earth was intentionally designed to express something about His character and nature. The Bible refers to physical things like trees, water, wind and animals to communicate spiritual truths to us. Likewise, our experiences of hunger, thirst, fatigue and illness are metaphors demonstrating our spiritual needs and condition. This is not a random coincidence, but purposeful. Consider the lion and the lamb — God created them deliberately, knowing they'd one day teach us about Jesus.

God was just as deliberate when He crafted your sexuality.

You were not created with sexual organs and desires just so you could get married and have babies. The whole drama of your sexuality, including singleness, marriage and procreation, are pieces of the larger picture.

Made for Intimacy

The Christian tradition that sex was made for marriage explains sexuality in a such a narrow manner that it leaves singles confused. If sex is for marriage, why do you as a single man or woman have such strong sexual desires? Why doesn't God take these longings away until He brings a spouse? And why would He care if you have sex with someone to whom you're not married?

How do we answer these questions? By realizing that God created sexuality to help us understand covenant love. Covenant love goes beyond romantic feelings or even the joy of close friendship. This love is based on a promise that cannot be broken, and this is God's love for His people. The overarching message of the Bible is God's covenant love — that a holy God pursues us with sacrificial, passionate love to bring us into fellowship with himself. Your sexuality is a profound tangible reminder of this truth. Here's how:

- Sexual desire invites you to pursue covenant.
- Sexual intimacy within marriage is the celebration of covenant.
- Sexual faithfulness is the promise of covenant.

For singles, that first point is the most important: Sexual desire invites you to pursue covenant.

Sexual Desire's Invitation

I've had the opportunity to interact with a lot of young adults. For most of these men and women, sexual desire represents a major struggle. They want to stop looking at porn and stop masturbating. They wonder if it's a big deal to sleep with someone they're dating. They want to know how to push "pause" on sexual feelings. Because their sexual drive seems to create so much drama, temptation and shame, it's often viewed as a bad thing. Matt Chandler said it this way:

> **Sometimes I meet young men who despair of their sexual appetite and say things like, "I just want God to take this away from me!" And I always say, "You really don't."**

What they should want God to do is empower their discipline and strength to be obedient, because sexual desire is a gift. We shouldn't ask God to take one of his gifts away from us.

We have to remember that sexual desire is not only a good thing, but a God thing. The Creator intentionally gave you the longings you have to share your life and body with another person.

In every one of us, Satan has twisted and tainted these desires so that they either represent selfish pursuit or shameful restraint. But this was not God's design from the beginning. Our sexual desire was created to remind us that we were made for intimacy. Not for a hookup or for sexual release looking at a computer screen, but for the sacrificial, life-giving intimacy represented by the marriage covenant.

Marriage's Metaphor

For most Christians, sexual desire will eventually lead us to the covenant vows of marriage. Largely because of sexual and romantic longings, we will sacrifice time, money and our vocational goals to pursue love. This is a good thing! In one respect, sexual longings "trick" us into making a lifelong promise that will ask far more from us than we anticipate. But in working out this covenant promise over a lifetime, we relationally and physically live out the metaphor of how God loves His people and how Jesus loves His bride.

But the marriage relationship is only a picture of true intimacy for which we were created. Marriage is not the answer for your loneliness; it is a metaphor of the answer. This is why marriage, as great as it may be, will ultimately fail to satisfy your deepest longings to be known and loved.

Why do you think there will be no marriage in heaven? Because in the reality of true intimacy with God, we will no longer need the metaphor.

Think of a time when you were describing to a friend what a foreign food tasted like. How would you describe a kiwi to someone who has never tasted it? You might explain that it tastes like a mixture between a melon and a strawberry with the texture of a peach. Once your friend has actually tasted a kiwi, your description will seem vaguely true, but lacking. You wouldn't continue with endless explanations of how kiwi tastes because now your friend knows in much greater detail than you could ever describe. This is how we need to view marriage (and sex within marriage). It is an approximation of something infinitely greater. Whether or not we are married, the metaphor isn't the point. We are called to strive for the real thing — intimate knowledge and fellowship with God.

The apostle Paul, a single man, wrote about the spiritual significance of marriage. I wonder if his relationship with Jesus was so intimate that he didn't need the "picture." Perhaps because he had tasted the real thing, he understood both the holiness of marriage as a metaphor but also how it paled in comparison to living with and for Christ Jesus. He kept reminding the early church that life would be found in intimately knowing Jesus.

Trading the Lesser for the Greater

Many Christians have bought into a cheap version of sex, even within marriage. Sex is not just about personal fulfillment and the satisfaction of your sexual desire. It's a call to something infinitely greater. It is a physical reminder that we were never meant to live in isolation and selfish pleasure. We were created for promise, for vulnerability, and for the pursuit and exchange of love that compels us to give ourselves away.

As a single person, you are invited to give yourself away through self-denial and service to the family of God. Your unmet sexual longings and needs are a physical reminder that you were meant for intimacy — ultimately intimacy with God. But please don't think that finding the right person will be the end of unmet longings or self-denial for the sake of Christ. Marriage, as Paul wrote, carries its own demands, distractions and disappointments. Even within the Garden of Eden before the Fall, Adam did not complete Eve. She wanted more and needed more.

Your sexuality was created to teach you about a faithful God ... about longing for Him, the pursuit of Him, the joy of Him and the promise of Him. Don't get so distracted by the metaphor that you miss the real thing for which your heart longs.

LET'S GET PRACTICAL

STUFF TO DO:

- Spend time with God so that He can change *you*, renew *your* mind and, like David, point out in *you* what is offensive, so that He can guide you on the way everlasting (Psalm 25:5, Psalm 139:23–24, Romans 12:2).
- Take it one day at a time and install God's truth into the hearts of your children bit by bit, by being positive and truthful, and by pointing them to God's ultimate plan.
- Teach them how to take their mistakes and failures to a loving Father who is always willing to forgive, heal, and restore. Lead by example.
- Don't just talk PURITY—live it, explain it, teach it, show it.
- And yes, do the bow tie and the promise ring as well; I think it's awesome.

STUFF TO TALK ABOUT:

- GOOD AND HEALTHY CHOICES: Talk to your kids often about what good and healthy choices are when it comes to sexuality and purity. Ask questions about how to dress and talk, which movies to watch, and music to listen to, and about friends and behaviors. Let them make the connections of what is good, kind, and acceptable. Explain that purity covers all areas of our lives and give examples. Just remember to not be legalistic about it. Raise your children with the knowledge that their sexual feelings are normal and healthy, but point those feelings towards God's original plan, which is marriage.

- DANGERS: Talk to them often about certain dangers, such as images of naked people or images of people having sex. They will come across it at school. Talk about it and tell them what to do if someone wants to show them such pictures. Tell them why it is dangerous and what God says about it. Prepare them for when it happens. (See *Chapter 6: Prepare Them for Puberty.*)

- FRUIT OF THE SPIRIT: Discuss the fruit of the Spirit (Galatians 5:22) and how it can help them to discern and identify an impure lifestyle. For example, faithfulness: Discuss what it means, what God says about it and what it looks like in a marriage, as well as what a marriage without faithfulness will look like.

- DIFFERENCES: Have talks about kids and adults who are different from us, who believe different things, who look different and behave differently. Be gracious and non-judgmental in your attitude.

- CERTAIN CONCEPTS: If your kids are still little, concepts such as honesty, obedience and kindness can be discussed. For example, when you see someone drop their wallet or if the cashier gives you too much change, what do you do? Do you take it for yourself or do you return it to the other person? That provides an opportunity for a conversation about honesty and what the consequences can be if you are dishonest. The cashier can get into trouble if he or she doesn't have the correct amount of money in the till at the end of the day, or the man who dropped his wallet won't have money to buy food for his family. Modeling honesty is modeling purity.

- METAPHORS: When they are a bit older, start introducing God's covenant relationship with us and how marriage was designed as a beautiful metaphor to reflect that covenant. Explain the symbolism and metaphors in the Bible and God's intentionality to them. In the beginning you can use easy examples such as who the Lion and the Lamb is, what wine and bread symbolize, and the meaning of the parables. Later you can go into more detail about more difficult concepts.

RECOMMENDED RESOURCES:

- *Rethinking Sexuality – God's Design and Why It Matters*, by Juli Slattery
- *SEX: Discovering Real Love in a World of Counterfeits*, a compilation by Bordon Books
- *Moral Revolution: The Naked Truth About Sexual Purity*, by Kris Valloton and Jason Valloton
- *Hooked*, by Joe S. McIlhaney and Freda McKissic Bush
- *When Good Kids Make Bad Choices*, by Elyse Fitzpatrick, James Newheiser and Laura Hendrickson

SCRIPTURES:

1 Samuel 16:7 But the Lord said to Samuel, "Do not consider his appearance or his height, for I have rejected him. The Lord does not look at the things people look at. People look at the outward appearance, but the Lord looks at the heart."

Proverbs 15:1 A gentle answer turns away wrath, but a harsh word stirs up anger.

Matthew 7:3–5 Why do you look at the speck of sawdust in your brother's eye and pay no attention to the plank in your own eye? How can you say to your brother, 'Let me take the speck out of your eye,' when all the time there is a plank in your own eye? You hypocrite, first take the plank out of your own eye, and then you will see clearly to remove the speck from your brother's eye.

Mark 7:21–23 For it is from within, out of a person's heart, that evil thoughts come—sexual immorality, theft, murder, adultery, greed, malice, deceit, lewdness, envy, slander, arrogance and folly. All these evils come from inside and defile a person.

Romans 12:1–2 Therefore, I urge you, brothers and sisters, in view of God's mercy, to offer your bodies as a living sacrifice, holy and pleasing to God— this is your true and proper worship. Do not conform to the pattern of this world, but be transformed by the renewing of your mind. Then you will be able to test and approve what God's will is—his good, pleasing and perfect will.

Galatians 5:22–23 But the fruit of the Spirit is love, joy, peace, forbearance, kindness, goodness, faithfulness, gentleness and self-control. Against such things there is no law.

Ephesians 5:4 Nor should there be obscenity, foolish talk or coarse joking, which are out of place, but rather thanksgiving.

1 Corinthians 6:19–20 Do you not know that your bodies are temples of the Holy Spirit, who is in you, whom you have received from God? You are not your own; you were bought at a price. Therefore honor God with your bodies.

Philippians 4:8 Finally, brothers and sisters, whatever is true, whatever is noble, whatever is right, whatever is pure, whatever is lovely, whatever is admirable—if anything is excellent or praiseworthy—think about such things.

Colossians 3:5 Put to death, therefore, whatever belongs to your earthly nature: sexual immorality, impurity, lust, evil desires and greed, which is idolatry.

1 Timothy 5:2 [Exhort] older women as mothers, and younger women as sisters, with absolute purity.

1 Peter 3:4 Rather, it should be that of your inner self, the unfading beauty of a gentle and quiet spirit, which is of great worth in God's sight.

CHAPTER 3

TEACH THEM SEXUAL SAFETY—THE SOONER THE BETTER

The prevalence of sexual abuse is on the rise. As a parent, you cannot afford to ignore it or not get involved. If you turn a blind eye to it, your children will be left vulnerable to sexual abuse. In this chapter you will learn how to minimize the risk of sexual abuse in your children's lives by putting a few things in place from a very young age. The younger you start teaching them, the better it is. Sexual abuse comes in many forms and can happen to anyone at any age.

You will also learn in this chapter how to teach them that they can keep themselves sexually safe as teenagers and adults by walking in their authority as children of God.

1. Teach them about BODY PARTS

Our bodies are fearfully and wonderfully made by a loving God! Always remember to be positive and to promote honor instead of shame when discussing these topics with your children.

Bath time is a great opportunity for these discussions. Make it fun and exciting. Ask the usual questions, such as, "What is this? Yes, it's your NOSE! Sniff, sniff, sniff. What a cute little nose you have! And what is this? Yes, this is your MOUTH! Talk, talk, talk. I love it when you tell me stories!" Then you keep going with the game and say, "And this is your [gender-appropriate private body part here]," and carry on asking about their knees, toes, and so on. (For example, "And this your vagina/penis! God made your vagina/penis very special and it is just right! Your vagina/penis is private. That means that it is just for *you*!") This is an amazing, non-threatening way to teach your children the correct names of their body parts and that all parts are special—without making a big deal out of it. Don't ignore their private parts or change your facial expression when talking about it. Start mastering that poker face! You are going to need it.

Also ask things such as, "What do your legs do? What do your fingers do? What does your buttocks do?" In this way, you can teach them that certain body parts are private. You are also showing them that you can handle talking about body parts without overreacting (this can be super important when they are older and need to share something with you).

It is important that your children know the correct names of their private parts, because it is common for predators to use silly, odd, or code names for these parts. When a child is taught the real names, it creates resistance for someone with ill motives. If you then hear your child calling a body part by a different name, you can ask, "And who told you that it is called a [wrong name]?" This way, you can find out who was talking to your child about his or her private parts. If something more happened, your child will be able to tell you which body part of the abuser was involved and where exactly the person touched him or her.

Words you can include in your conversation are 'public' and 'private'.

- 'Private' means: just for you; personal.
- 'Public' means: for other people as well.

Teach your children the following:

- Certain **body parts** are private, such as the vagina, penis, testicles, buttocks, testicles, breasts, and mouth.
- Certain **items** are private, such as underwear.
- Certain **places** are private, such as the toilet and the bathroom, and their beds.
- Certain **behaviors** are private, such as going to the toilet and taking a bath. Many schools have unisex dressing rooms. If that is the case at your child's school, ensure that they are wearing gym pants underneath their school clothes, and teach them to turn their backs to the opposite sex when undressing in the same room.

Children start developing their sense of privacy very early on and it needs to be respected. When your children start showing signs that they prefer dressing or bathing alone, you should respect it. But, in saying this, don't make a big deal out of it. Young children don't think sexually. It is about teaching them the principles of privacy and appropriateness in a fun, matter-of-fact way.

If, for instance, it happens that your child comes home and tells you that she saw Johnny's penis while changing for her swimming lesson, use it as an opportunity to chat about privacy, things she can do to show respect for others' privacy, and the fact that God made boys and girls different and special. Don't overreact or make a big deal out of it. You want your children to talk to you about these matters when they are teenagers. If she wants to ask questions about penises, she needs to know that you are a straight-faced, I-can-talk-about-a-penis mom, not a big-eyed, jaw-dropping, how-dare-you-mention-the-penis-word-and-by-the-way-*never*-kiss-a-boy mom.

2. Teach them about FEELINGS

We all have the right to feel safe anywhere at all times. Each word in this sentence is important! When you discuss this with your children, always remember to focus on the special body God gave each of us and that no one has the right to make anyone else feel unsafe, not even someone we know and trust.

WE ALL: Everyone, and that even includes the bully at school!

RIGHT: No one can take this away from you; you do not have to earn it; it belongs to you.

SAFE: Safe on a physical and emotional level.

ANYWHERE: No matter where you are and who you are with: At school, at home, in your room, in your bed—anywhere.

ALL TIMES: No matter what time of day or night, no matter what day of the week, school-day or weekend or holiday.

Teaching your children to identify feelings and emotions is a process and requires a lot of patience. This is a very important skill for them to master. It paves the way towards recognizing when they are in danger.

Keep it simple. Talk to your children about feelings of happiness and show them a picture of a smiling family or a kid having fun and laughing while playing. Do the same for different emotions.

Also ask them often to explain their own feelings to you. Try to put words to the emotions. For example, if your toddler is crying because you said he cannot visit his granny, tell him that you can see that he is feeling disappointed. (You can also use the words 'sad' or 'unhappy'.)

The difference between feeling safe and unsafe is an important lesson. Start this lesson by pointing out that it might be fun to feel a little scared sometimes, like when you are on a roller coaster or a high swing, or when you do something daring like speaking in front of people or acting on a stage. Those are all things that can be a bit scary!

"But what is the difference between *safe* scary and *unsafe* scary?"

Safe scary: Your child can *choose* to get on the roller coaster, high swing or skateboard and when to get off, any time he or she wants to. Your child has a choice and control, and there is a time limit.

Unsafe scary: When a situation is not safe, such as in the case of sexual abuse, the child usually has no choice in the matter. They have no control over what is happening to them and they cannot make it stop. It can continue with no end in sight.

Another important tool to teach your children is how they can recognize these feelings in their little bodies. Ask your children what they feel in their bodies when they feel scared. For instance, "Does your heart beat faster? Do you have butterflies in your tummy? Do you get goosebumps, or jelly knees, or feel shaky? Do you freeze?" Teach them that they should pay attention to it if they have these feelings. Their bodies are trying to tell them that a specific situation might not be safe.

This is a good time to teach them that they are the bosses of their own bodies and that each body has a personal space bubble. They can choose who they want to hug, kiss and high-five. They can choose who they allow into their personal space bubbles, such as mom, dad and siblings. Do not force your children to give hugs to people they don't want to hug. Also teach them that it is even possible that people in their personal bubble can make them feel unsafe, and that they can say, "No," or, "Stop," and move away.

A great board game I can recommend is the Smart Heart Board Game, which was developed by psychologists in South Africa. This game is a great tool to teach young ones to identify and communicate feelings, a skill that will foster mental health, and it helps to initiate conversations for them to talk about serious issues in a playful manner. It helps them to think independently. When we played this game with our children, I got to know a whole different side of them. Even my husband and I played it because it helps to facilitate communication.

3. Teach them about ACTION

Most children are taught to be respectful and kind, and that is good. It can, however, make it hard for them to resist a predator, especially if it is someone they know and trust, or if your child is a sweet, kind, soft-hearted, people-pleasing person. Teach them that they are allowed to be loud, aggressive, and even disrespectful if they feel physically or sexually unsafe. Assertiveness is a skill that must be practiced. Children need to hear from you as the parent that you will back them and support them in cases where they had to act out of the norm. It will give them more confidence to act when it is necessary.

You have to go into detail about when they should act. Name the body parts involved, as well as the actions of the predator. Teach them exactly when, where, and how they should not be touched or kissed by anyone else. For example, it's not okay if a grown-up asks a child to sit on his or her lap and starts rubbing the child's leg. The next time, the perpetrator might rub a little higher up and slowly progress to the genitals. The perpetrator might show the child pictures of naked people or expose him- or herself. All these situations need to be pointed out as typical predator behavior and grooming methods. Your children need to be aware of it so that they know what to do if this ever happens to them. The action steps you can teach them to take in such situations are: NO, GO, and TELL.

Teach your children how to say NO

First demonstrate a POLITE NO to them: "No, I do not want candy. No, I do not want to sit next to you. No, I am not going to walk with you."

Then show them an ASSERTIVE NO: "NO, I am not going to sit on your lap. NO, I am not going to the room/car/bushes with you." Show them how to use a more serious face and a louder voice. Let your children practice on you. In this way you can also teach them which types of questions from others require a more assertive NO.

Then, move on to an ANGRY NO. Stomp your feet, frown and lift your hand up in front of you, saying in a loud voice: "NO, LEAVE ME ALONE! NO, DO NOT TOUCH ME THERE! NO, STOP IT!"

Lastly, show them an EMERGENCY NO. This is where they have to shout, scream, run, fight, bite, and so on. (Might be fun to practice this one!)

When your children are teenagers, teach them how to look a boy or girl in the eye and say, "NO." Let them practice on you.

Teach them where to GO

GO, in this sense, means to get away as quickly as possible, like running away fast.

Explain to them where they can go: Another adult, a mom or dad with kids, a security guard, a teacher, or the like.

You can also teach them the concept of the **HELPING HAND**. This is a great tool to remind them of who they can go to. Assign the name of a trusted adult to each finger on one of your child's hands. You can even trace your child's hand on a paper and write down each of the five names. It must be people who are available, willing to listen, who will believe them and make them feel safe again, like mom or dad, a teacher, coach, or grandma.

While having these discussions with your children, also mention areas where they *should not* go at all, such as lonely roads, deserted public bathrooms, dark alleyways, or any place a stranger might invite them to. Sketch a scenario and start by using the words 'what if'. For example, "What if someone you don't know comes to you in the park and asks you to walk to his car with him to look at his new puppies?" Let them answer and correct them if necessary. They must learn to think before they decide. This is even hard for adults! Practice 'what if' with your children often.

Another example is when they are older and start going out with friends. Come up with a secret code they can text you if they feel unsafe, so that you can pick them up immediately (and without them committing social suicide). It can be something simple, like 'xxxx', something that their friends won't understand and that just looks like an innocent text to you. Make a deal that it's okay if they don't want to talk about it; you will pick them up immediately, no matter what, with no questions asked. They need to know that you are there for them when they need you, without any expectations and no matter the reason. It will be easier for them to confide in you when they are ready to talk about it later. Even if you smell alcohol, see that their pupils are dilated and look like two black marbles, or hear a soft cry from the back of the car, still honor the no-questions-asked deal. In this way, they know that they can trust you and that you will not freak out when they need you.

Teach them to TELL

Speaking up will be much easier for a child if sexual safety is discussed at home and is a regular part of your parenting. Remember, in most cases, abuse comes from a trusted adult, so speaking up can be very hard, especially if the child has been threatened. For example, "No one will believe you," or, "I will tell everyone that it was your fault," or, "You will be sent away," or, "If you tell anyone, I will hurt your [parents/little sister/etc.]." Role play often with your children and teach them that any time they feel unsafe—even if it is with their favorite uncle, teacher, coach, etc.—they must still say NO, then GO and TELL. Always.

Teach them that they can always talk to someone about it, no matter what it is. If you as the parent can be that person, all the better.

Children must also know the difference between **safe secrets** and **unsafe secrets**. An example of a safe secret is a surprise, like if it is daddy's birthday: "We're having a surprise party for daddy. You are not allowed to tell him!" This type of secret lasts only for a short time, others also know about it, it is fun and exciting, no one feels scared or uncomfortable or unsafe, and it has a happy outcome. You can describe an unsafe secret as a secret where the child might have been threatened and has no choice about telling, the secret lasts a long time, and is accompanied by scary and uncomfortable feelings. It is important to teach your children that whenever there is a secret, there is also a big possibility of danger. So always TELL.

The concept of **safe touches** and **unsafe touches** is vital to talk about. It is important to teach your children the difference. Safe and appropriate touches CAN change to unsafe, worrying touches. Explain to your children that NO ONE is allowed to touch or kiss them without their permission. Some adults don't know the rules about touching, so teach your child to speak up and TELL. If touching gives them scary feelings or signs in their bodies, it's not their fault and they should TELL someone on their helping hand.

NO, GO, TELL. Easy to remember!

4. Teach your children about CONSENT

We must teach our kids, especially our boys, about asking permission before we hug, kiss, or touch one another's bodies. Below is an example of how I would tackle this conversation.

Johnny: "Mom, yesterday I hugged Sarah at school, and she hugged me back, but today when I wanted to hug her, she seemed a bit weird about it."

Me: "Did you ask her if she wanted or needed a hug?"

Johnny: "No, not really. I did once, a long time ago!"

Me: "That's good. But here's the thing: You must ask *every new time*. Ask with your words, not with your hands or arms. Every time you want to give someone a hug, you can say, 'Hey, Sarah, may I give you a hug?' Or ask, 'May I hold your hand?' Her 'yes' of yesterday might not be a 'yes' today! Her 'yes' of 10 minutes ago might even change into a 'no'. And that's okay. Sometimes you also change your mind about things. You must learn to listen to what she is saying without words. For example, if she says, 'Yes, you can give me a hug,' but it looks like she actually doesn't want a hug, then you must respect that and rather not give her a hug."

Johnny: "Really?"

Me: "Yup! And she should also ask for your permission if she wants to give you a hug or a kiss!"

Johnny: "MOM! Gross. I'm gonna go now."

Me: "Thank goodness!"

5. Teach your children to TAKE AUTHORITY

As your children grow up, they might find themselves in situations where they feel unsafe. Even as adults we sometimes feel unsafe. This can be for a variety of reasons: Walking home alone, feeling uncomfortable with certain people around you at a party, the hairs on your neck standing on end because of the way someone looked at you in the mall, or even feeling unsafe when you are alone with someone you know, such as your boss, a colleague, a teacher, or even a pastor. What can happen if your child finds him- or herself in one of the scenarios and you are not around?

Whenever you get the feeling of being unsafe, the Holy Spirit is trying to tell you something. It is a cue to act immediately, for yourself, and also for your children. Teach them to do the same, because you will not always be around when they are in compromising or unsafe places. We must empower our children to go to their Heavenly Father when they feel unsafe, no matter their age.

I was 12 years old when a family member asked my dad to assist at a bridal exhibition. It was held at a well-known hotel in our area. My dad had three daughters and saw this occasion as an opportunity for us to make some pocket money. As soon as my sisters and I arrived at the exhibition, eagerly looking for the wedding gown sections, we were approached by an older gentleman, probably around 50 years old. He was advertising his limousine service to the brides-to-be and he wanted us to stand next to the limousine and hand out his flyers. Not a lot of time went by before he asked us to get into the limousine with him. I remember looking for my dad, but he was busy working somewhere else and was not around. The situation didn't feel right to us, but because there were so many people around and he wanted all three of us in the car, and the fact that my dad had shared a few jokes with this man earlier, we decided to get in.

The car had tinted windows, and he closed the door after all of us had climbed in. He started talking about how we should shorten our skirts to attract more customers. He praised our bodies and told us that we should be underwear models for the 'other' business he was running, and he talked a lot about his riches and success. He reckoned we would be perfect models. I remember how his hungry eyes looked us up and down – my sisters were about 9 and 11 years old. I started feeling very uncomfortable and I remember looking at his shoes as he was piling on the compliments of how amazing we would look in photographs. At first, I didn't think much of it, and I even felt flattered. But the funny, niggling-red-light feeling didn't go away. As I listened to how he was trying to convince us to show more leg, I noticed something about his shoes. It drew my attention because it didn't fit in with his tuxedo. The shoes were worn and dirty; they looked old and damaged. I looked more closely at his suit and realized that it, too, was worn and wrinkled. His white shirt was not so white anymore and had a few brown stains. When my eyes moved up to his bow tie that was frayed at the edges, something in me started screaming that we should get out of the car. I looked up into his eyes and what I saw there was evil, ugly, and dangerous. I tried to move closer to my sisters, and I noticed him moving closer to the door, as if to lock it. The bald spot on his head, covered with a few sparse long flaps of hair, was starting to show drops of perspiration, and his weird smile made every hair on my body stand on end. That was when I heard a voice in my spirit that said, "Get out now!" I grabbed my sisters' hands and said in a stern voice, "We have to go." I literally pushed my sisters out of the limousine. My sudden reaction had caught him by surprise, and he couldn't stop us. We got out and ran to find my dad.

But I didn't tell him about what had happened.

Later that day I saw my dad talking to him again, smiling from ear to ear, lending his ears out to this man lavishing compliments on his daughters. He even told my dad that we would be great underwear models! My dad didn't realize the danger—he was too flattered and naive. My dad never thought ill of anyone.

I was upset for a very long time after that day. I wasn't upset with the creepy man—I was upset with my dad. He wasn't there to protect us, and he didn't notice the danger. He was so flattered that a 'rich' businessman was interested in his pretty daughters that it blinded him. Could he not see that the man's clothes did not suit his words? That most of the fake leather on his black pointy shoes was scratched off from wear and tear? Rich people don't wear shoes like that! Could he not sense the pedophilic lust pouring from this man? Why didn't it bother him that an old guy wanted to photograph his daughters in underwear? Where was he when we were in that car? And why did I never tell him about it? Maybe I thought that he wouldn't believe me. I mean, the man was boasting about his riches, his connections and his 'eye for beauty'… My dad's ego was blinded by words of praise about his three beautiful girls. My dad was very impressed with the man, and because he had an outgoing, social personality and a very trusting nature, he had no idea that this man wasn't just grooming *us*, but *him* as well. It resulted in me losing my trust in my dad's ability to protect us.

And it hurt.

It took me a long time to forgive him. I buried my disappointment in my father very deep in my heart, but stuff like that has a way of revealing itself. In my late teens it became clear that our relationship was damaged. I was rude, disrespectful, angry, resentful, and overall horrible to him. I rejected his affection and tried my best to avoid him. At the time I had no idea why I was treating him like that. It was only years later that I became aware that the issues between us came from that incident. God showed me this splinter in my heart at a church camp 12 years later. I cried for three days on end. I eventually forgave my dad at the age of 24 (he still had no clue), and our relationship changed completely.

The point of my story is that the enemy wanted to steal, kill, and destroy that day. The Holy Spirit warned me. I recognized His voice and got out of the car. My sisters and I were saved from something that could have caused a lot of damage. Unfortunately, the enemy did succeed in one thing that day: I believed his lies about my dad. For years I blamed my dad for not protecting us that day. (He was completely unaware of the situation; he was busy working somewhere else and he was just being himself—someone with a trusting, fun-loving nature, with normal human flaws, and without superhero powers and laser eyes that can see everything.) But what I didn't realize was that when my earthly father 'failed' me, my Heavenly Father was right there, protecting us.

And that is why it is so very important that we teach our children to hear God's voice, to know who is their Father that sees everything, and to take authority so that the enemy can flee. You will not always be around, and even if you are, you can also be blinded. We have to teach our children to recognize God's voice and to use their authority.

A great book that I can recommend is *Journey* by Lisa Max. It is a wonderful tool that will show you how to practically teach your child to hear God's voice.

6. Teach your children to HEAL

This is the hard part. Healing is something you have no control over when it comes to someone else. It's something you can model, but you have no control over your child's healing. Prevention is better than cure, so that is why we try to equip our children in the first place. If your family is in the unfortunate position of dealing with a child affected by sexual abuse, there are a few steps you can take to help them. The way you respond is crucial.

Learn to recognize when your child is acting out of the ordinary. That is usually a big indication that something is wrong. Certain behaviors, such as sudden bed-wetting, aggressive behavior, and hectic mood swings can indicate that there is something that needs to be talked about. Don't ignore it. It can be nothing, but rather check and affirm your love and support, reminding your child that he or she can talk to you about anything, no matter what it is, and that you can help.

Tell your child the following:

- I believe you.
- I am glad you told me.
- I am sorry that this happened to you.
- It is not your fault.
- Abuse is wrong and it must stop.
- Your body belongs to you.
- People you love and trust sometimes do bad things and it is not okay.
- What happens to the abuser now is not your fault.
- I need to speak to other adults in order to help you.

What you should do if any form of abuse has taken place:

- Please get professional help for your child.
- Listen to your child.
- Talk to your child often, love him or her, and encourage him or her to talk (especially to a counselor).
- Talk to other parents who went through the same thing with their children.
- Pray for your child and with your child.
- A wonderful book that can be a powerful tool in your toolbox is *Heart Splinters* by Lisa Max. This book is about how to resolve childhood hurts during childhood, so that it doesn't affect them as adults.

The enemy wants to steal, kill, and destroy. Don't give him a foothold through bitterness, anger and hate. Fight him. Protect your children. Ask

God for wisdom. Don't leave them vulnerable; make them resilient and strong. God's Word is like a two-edged sword. Use it and teach your kids how to use it as well. Our bodies are God's temple; the *King of kings* lives in it! Let's get this right. Be intentional with your children every day. You can do anything through Christ who strengthens you. And don't forget that!

LET'S GET PRACTICAL

STUFF TO DO:

- Some children are very detail-oriented and would like to know how the body works. Do your research properly and have simplified, annotated diagrams or medical illustrations of the body at hand. Keep it simple and age appropriate. Start making a collection of pictures and diagrams on your computer that you can add to your discussions.

- To be aware of what you are feeling is something that even adults struggle with. From now on, always try to put a name to a feeling. Try to label your own emotions, as well as your children's. This can be done by daily discussions. You can ask questions at the dinner table, such as, "You had to tell your class about your holiday today. Did you feel a bit nervous before the time? It can be a bit scary standing in front of anyone, isn't it? My heart always beats faster! I feel it here in my neck. But you know what? I bet you everyone felt exactly like you did!" You can even ask, "Tell me about your favorite part of the day," and then try to label the positive feelings, such as excited, silly, happy, or funny. Then you can ask, "Tell me about the worst part of your day," and again try to label the feelings, for example feeling embarrassed, awkward, alone, stupid, or sad.

For example, "So you are saying that the worst part of your day was when you fell, and your friend laughed at you? How did that make you feel?" Young kids will not be able to tell you that the feeling is 'humiliated', but take the opportunity to teach them a new word as well. You can say, "I think you probably felt humiliated. That means that they made you feel silly/shy/stupid and it hurt your feelings when your friend laughed at you. Let's say the big word together: HUMILIATED. Not a nice feeling, is it?" You can then go on to tell them how you would deal with the situation.

- Try to get to words such as uncomfortable, scared, uneasy, shame, guilt, and so on. These are feelings that can describe an unsafe situation for a child.

- One emotion per day. Keep it simple. Repeat it often.

- Practice saying NO, in all its forms, on a regular basis, BY USING BODY LANGUAGE. Let them repeat the statement NO, GO, TELL by using their bodies.

  NO = Shake the head
  GO = Run on the spot
  TELL = Move the hand like a talking mouth

- Make the HELPING HAND by using craft materials.

- Teach them to hear God's voice and how to take authority. Practice this throughout their childhood so that it becomes second nature.

- Invent your own body board game. Find simplified diagrams and pictures of body parts on the computer. Be creative!

STUFF TO TALK ABOUT:

It's never too late. Start tonight!

- Initiate an informal conversation about how God made our bodies.
- Discuss funny names and nicknames, but most importantly, the real names for different body parts.
- If your children are older, make sure that they know the correct names. Depending on their ages, medical diagrams can be a good tool.

- Before your children hit puberty, make sure they also know the correct terms for the unseen areas, such as uterus, fallopian tubes, urethra, cervix, rectum, prostate, etc. Throw in the patella and clavicle while you are at it. If they know about 'pecs', 'glutes', hamstrings, and 'quads' (words that are often used in sports or gym circles), then they ought to know where the vagina ends and the cervix starts. This will help you when you need to explain more complex information later on.
- Regularly discuss emotions and feelings, including feeling safe versus feeling unsafe.
- Practice talking about uncomfortable things and unsafe secrets and touches.
- Talk about where they can GO to be safe and where they should NOT go.
- Remind them often that asking for permission to hug or kiss someone else is good manners. If the person says no, your child might feel a bit sad, but explain to them that it is important to respect other people's boundaries. Not everyone likes hugs.
- Explain to them that it is also okay to reject even the most polite request for a hug if they are not comfortable with it. Empower them to say NO, as discussed previously in this chapter under point number three, *Teach them about ACTION*.
- Talk about recognizing God's voice and practice it. Let it become a habit to ask God what to do first, before you ask anybody else.

RECOMMENDED RESOURCES:

- Books: *The Swimsuit Lesson* by Jon Holsten, *Journey* and *Heart Splinters* by Lisa Max
- SMART HEART board game – www.smartheartboardgame.com/smart-heart-board-game

SCRIPTURES:

<u>Authority</u>

Psalm 46:10 He says, "Be still, and know that I am God; I will be exalted among the nations, I will be exalted in the earth."

Matthew 28:18 Then Jesus came to them and said, "All authority in heaven and on earth has been given to me."

Luke 10:19 I have given you authority to trample on snakes and scorpions and to overcome all the power of the enemy; nothing will harm you.

Acts 5:29 Peter and the other apostles replied: "We must obey God rather than human beings!"

Hebrews 4:12 For the word of God is alive and active. Sharper than any double-edged sword, it penetrates even to dividing soul and spirit, joints and marrow; it judges the thoughts and attitudes of the heart.

James 4:7 Submit yourselves, then, to God. Resist the devil, and he will flee from you.

1 John 3:8 The one who does what is sinful is of the devil, because the devil has been sinning from the beginning. The reason the Son of God appeared was to destroy the devil's work.

1 John 4:4 You, dear children, are from God and have overcome them, because the one who is in you is greater than the one who is in the world.

<u>Protection and safety</u>

Psalm 46:1 God is our refuge and strength, an ever-present help in trouble.

Psalm 91:1–2 Whoever dwells in the shelter of the Most High will rest in the shadow of the Almighty. I will say of the Lord, "He is my refuge and my fortress, my God, in whom I trust."

Psalm 138:7 Though I walk in the midst of trouble, you preserve my life. You stretch out your hand against the anger of my foes; with your right hand you save me.

Proverbs 2:11 Discretion will protect you, and understanding will guard you.

Proverbs 4:6 Do not forsake wisdom, and she will protect you; love her, and she will watch over you.

Proverbs 11:14 For lack of guidance a nation falls, but victory is won through many advisers.

Nahum 1:7a The Lord is good, a refuge in times of trouble.

2 Thessalonians 3:3 But the Lord is faithful, and he will strengthen you and protect you from the evil one.

Healing

2 Chronicles 7:14–15 … if my people, who are called by my name, will humble themselves and pray and seek my face and turn from their wicked ways, then I will hear from heaven, and I will forgive their sin and will heal their land. Now my eyes will be open and my ears attentive to the prayers offered in this place.

Psalm 73:26 My flesh and my heart may fail, but God is the strength of my heart and my portion forever.

Psalm 147:3 He heals the brokenhearted and binds up their wounds.

Proverbs 17:22 A cheerful heart is good medicine, but a crushed spirit dries up the bones.

Isaiah 40:29 He gives strength to the weary and increases the power of the weak.

Isaiah 41:10 So do not fear, for I am with you; do not be dismayed, for I am your God. I will strengthen you and help you; I will uphold you with my righteous right hand.

Isaiah 53:4–5 Surely he took up our pain and bore our suffering, yet we considered him punished by God, stricken by him, and afflicted. But he was pierced for our transgressions, he was crushed for our iniquities; the punishment that brought us peace was on him, and by his wounds we are healed.

Jeremiah 30:17 "But I will restore you to health and heal your wounds," declares the Lord,
"because you are called an outcast, Zion for whom no one cares."

John 14:27 Peace I leave with you; my peace I give you. I do not give to you as the world gives. Do not let your hearts be troubled and do not be afraid.

Philippians 4:19 And my God will meet all your needs according to the riches of his glory in Christ Jesus.

James 5:6 You have condemned and murdered the innocent one, who was not opposing you.

1 Peter 2:24 "He himself bore our sins" in his body on the cross, so that we might die to sins and live for righteousness; "by his wounds you have been healed."

Revelation 21:4 He will wipe every tear from their eyes. There will be no more death or mourning or crying or pain, for the old order of things has passed away.

Chapter 4

Teach Them the Goodness of Sexuality— It's the Best Thing Ever

God made sex, and it is good. God made sexual feelings, and it is good. God made marriage and families, and it is good. So when we discuss and teach our children these things, remember: IT IS GOOD. Remember that, especially when they mess up! It gives you a fantastic teachable moment to impart grace, forgiveness, love, and biblical direction.

Dr. Darleen Edwards-Meyer uses an easy model in her programs to assist parents in discussing sexuality with their children. It is called 'The 7 P's'. If you keep the 7 P's in mind and include it in your discussions as much as possible, it will guide your discussions in the right direction and help you to not leave out important information. It will assist you in handling questions and initiating discussions in an uplifting and positive way.

1. Memorize the 7 P's

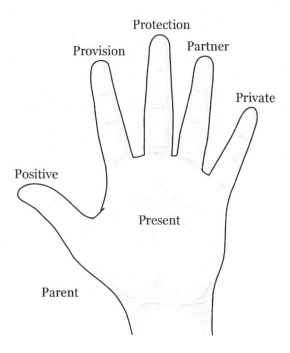

Parent: God is our Father, just as you are the **parent** of your child. Look at your hand as a whole and remember that just as you love your child, God loves him or her even more. He holds us in His hands just like we hold our kids in ours.

Present: Open your hand. Inside is a very special gift that God gave us: A **present** from God for our wedding day. It is the gift of you – your mind, body, and soul. God created only one of you, and because you are so special, you should be extra careful about giving yourself as a gift through sexual intimacy. Your sexuality is a 'wedding gift' from God to be opened on your wedding day. You don't open a gift before the time! If you insist on a marriage commitment before giving the gift of yourself, you are demanding the respect and honor you truly deserve. The person who truly loves you will value your gift enough to wait for it. This present was God's idea and it made Him happy to give it to us, because this special gift is a symbol of His commitment to and covenant with us: a blood covenant. Personally, the fact that God gave us something that can make us feel so good and gives us so much pleasure, makes me want to get to know Him even more. This gift is rare and exquisite; it is one of a kind. It is priceless. You own this gift, and you are in charge of protecting it and choosing the one who will be worthy of receiving it.

Positive: Make a thumbs-up sign with your hand. This means that it is **positive**. Our sexuality, sexual feelings, marriage, and families are all good and positive. This should remind you to handle questions and discussions regarding sexuality with a positive attitude. Our bodies are 'fearfully and wonderfully made'! (Psalm 139:14)

Provision: Your index finger is for God's **provision**. It is pointing you in the right direction. God gave us this special present for various reasons: It provides us with intimacy that we should only share with our own spouse, it bonds us to that one and only person in a special way, it was made to give us pleasure, and it was created so that we can have children. God provided us with an emotionally safe, lifelong commitment space where we can express sexual desire freely, often, and safely in order to enrich one another.

Protection: The middle finger, the longest one, stands out above the rest. This finger reminds us of God's **protection**. There is a reason for God's boundaries: it is for our protection. The safest way to enjoy our sexuality at its fullest is by honoring the boundaries that God puts in place. Promiscuity, adultery, casual sex, fornication (and the list goes on) never have a happy ending (excuse the pun)! The world is full of the heartbreaking consequences of being slaves to our own lust. Sex bonds two people together, not just physically, but emotionally, mentally, and spiritually. A break-up rips that bond apart, causing extreme pain. And we all know how damaged people deal with pain: depression, sadness, substance abuse, numbness, promiscuity, not being able to connect emotionally again, fear, suicide... there is a long list.

Partner: The ring finger symbolizes that word **partner**. This is to remind you to always include the concept that your children's sexuality is for the special person they will marry one day: That one person they will commit to for life, the one person who will be willing to commit to them for life, the one they will be in covenant with—their spouse.

Private: The pinky is to remind us that our bodies are **private** and cannot just be given to anyone. It is a form of sexual safety—sexual safety is more than just protecting ourselves from sexual abuse. It is also for protecting us from ourselves.

Memorize the 7 P's to assist you in any discussions regarding sexuality. (For examples of how to include the 7 P's in your discussions, refer to *Chapter 5: How to Handle Those Uncomfortable Questions*.) Try to use most of the P's wherever you can. As you practice it you will see how this model successfully gives your children a positive vision for their futures, as you are always pointing them back to God and His original plan. It will also assist you in your manner: Always be positive and show honor to your children and their questions. By initiating discussions often with the 7 P's involved, and by answering questions truthfully, you are teaching your children that their sexuality was God's great idea and is, therefore, a good thing. By using the 7 P's you put their sexuality in its proper place, pointing it towards the God who made it.

Handling your children's questions can be a very difficult task, especially if they ask where babies come from... while you are driving them to the movies. And that at the age of five! I almost rolled the car, not expecting that question for another few years! Fortunately, I had the 7 P's to back me up, so I was prepared.

I also had the foundation laid, having already explained to them about eggs and seeds after they asked questions about chicken eggs, tadpoles, and nature shows. These questions and discussions provided great teaching moments before the BIG question was asked so randomly. The way in which you, as a parent, answer their questions makes such a big impact in their little minds. It is so important to get the message across to them that our sexuality is good, even if they have no idea what it is yet.

"WHAT IS THIS FOR, MOMMY?" When your child asks this in the middle of a shop, condom or tampon box held sky high for all to see, it might be difficult to answer while navigating your fully stacked shopping trolley through long queues, with everyone being able to overhear your conversation. You can answer something along the lines of, "I would love to answer your question, but there are a few things that I have to explain, so we can talk about it at home." Then be ready to answer it in simple terms. (*See Chapter 5: How to Handle Those Uncomfortable Questions.*) But we all probably have at least one child who will insist on an answer right then and there. In this case, keep it short: "Nose bleeds. Now wait until we are at home, otherwise I will have to show you how it works!" (The answer about nosebleeds can lay a good foundation to explain how tampons work.)

Build a vision in them for the future with regard to their sexuality: it is something seriously good, precious, and amazing to wait for. Imagine if all parents could do this... Imagine if your child can marry someone who was raised like this. Wow!

2. Love, respect and accept your children as they are

How you give and receive love directly influences your children's sexuality and whether they will view sexuality as good or bad. There are countless examples to give of parents who struggle with giving and receiving love (for various reasons), and the result is children who grow up unloved and confused, with disastrous consequences throughout all areas of their lives. The consequences are especially prevalent in their own relationships. Give your love unconditionally and freely—to your spouse and your kids. They shouldn't feel that they should earn it. If you need help in this area, do what you have to do to sort yourself out, because your spouse and your children need to feel loved and respected EVERY SINGLE DAY.

Messages are subconsciously being sent to your children in your home every day from birth. Did you accept your child's gender, unique talents, and temperament? Are your kids witnessing a loving marriage? Do you model respect for your spouse and your friends? If you are a single parent, are you modeling love and respect in your friendships? Do you bad-mouth your ex-husband or -wife? I once read about a divorced man who continued to surprise his ex-wife with flowers and a gift on her birthday. People questioned him about it and his answer was that his sons are witnessing how he treats their mother, even though they are not married anymore. He wants them to see how they should treat a woman and he knows that his behavior will influence how they act in their future relationships. What a wise dad!

Our behavior, what we say and how we say it all have an influence on our children's sexuality and how they will view their future relationships. You want to instill in them that marriage is a wonderful institution, designed by a loving God, and that it is something to look forward to. Give them a good vision for their future, even if you are a single parent and even if you have been hurt. Your kids' future relationships deserve it.

3. Teach your children to accept their bodies, its reactions and functions

When your child is exploring his or her own body, curiously discovering all its different parts and sometimes playing with it, it's not wrong or bad. Don't slap your child's hand away when it goes to their private parts, but rather take their hand away gently without making a big deal of it. When your child can understand a bit more, you can tell him or her that the penis or vagina is private and that it can make other people uncomfortable if he or she touches it in public. Remember that sexual feelings are natural, and it feels good. We don't want our children to feel guilty about having these feelings, but it needs to be put in the right place. Talking about it and including the 7 P's is a way to do just that. (Of course, there can be instances where you might be concerned about excessive touching, and in such cases, make sure that there isn't a medical reason, for instance itching. Or maybe you just have to change a few habits. Bored children with no intellectual stimulation or emotionally deprived children can get up to all kinds of things. If you are worried, get professional help.)

You might have to address certain games, such as doctor-doctor, or if they show one another their private parts. This presents a great opportunity to discuss which types of games are not acceptable. Be gentle but firm. Explain to them clearly what is not allowed and suggest healthy, appropriate alternatives. (See *Chapter 5: How to Handle Those Uncomfortable Questions*.)

When your children are older, it is essential to talk about sexual feelings. These feelings are natural, and it needs to be handled correctly, not ignored. Your children need to know that they can discuss these things with you openly. You need to teach them that they don't have to act on their sexual feelings and how to practice self-control. Hettie Brits, a South African author and CEO of Evergreen Parenting, says that teaching your children self-control when they are still small is vital to prepare them for future situations that WILL come their way, where they will need self-control. If they can learn when they are young to accept it and control themselves when you say, "NO MORE ICE CREAM," they will be in a much better position to control themselves when they are in compromising situations one day, or if they are exposed to peer pressure. They might even have to put out an already half-smoked cigarette, walk out halfway through a movie or get dressed halfway through being undressed!

4. Toilet training must be fun and educational

You are even teaching your children about the goodness of sexuality during toilet training! The same parts that get used when going to the toilet are the parts associated with sex. We don't want children to be embarrassed or feel shame about these parts of their bodies. To use the potty is a natural thing and should be handled with love, patience, and acceptance. Don't shame them for accidents or if they progress slower than their peers. Always be positive and uplifting. And remember to praise them when they get it right! Keep it fun, exciting, and positive.

Make sure that they are ready for potty training before you start, because some children will be slower with this than others. Boys are sometimes a bit slower than girls when it comes to potty training. Be patient—it takes a while! Look out for signs that show that they are ready, like the following:

They…

- can follow simple instructions
- understand and use words about using the potty
- can make the connection between the urge to wee or poop and using the potty for it
- are able to diaper dry for two hours or more
- can get to the potty, sit on it for long enough, and then get off the potty
- are capable of pulling down diapers, disposable training pants or underwear
- show an interest in using the potty or wearing underwear.

LET'S GET PRACTICAL

STUFF TO DO:

- Memorize the 7 P's and practice how to use it in different scenarios. Come up with questions that you might want to think through before answering it and practice with other parents. To see an example of how to use the 7 P's, read *Chapter 5: How to Handle Those Uncomfortable Questions.*
- Love, respect and accept your spouse and children as they are.
- Teach your child to accept his or her body, its functions, and its reactions. Put sexual feelings in its correct place by discussions during teachable moments.
- Lay the foundation early on. Before you can discuss sex, your children need to know a few basics, such as the difference between boys and girls, eggs, and seeds, and so on. Slowly build up to sex— think of it as 'sexual education foreplay' if you will!
- By the time that your children reach the age of seven, you should start telling them about sex—before they hear about it at school. Because they WILL hear about it at school, and you will not be there. The window of time when they believe every word that comes from your mouth (and ask a thousand questions) becomes smaller the older they get. So get in there and open that 'file' in their heads first! Everything they hear after that will be judged by what you have taught them. Be the first to tell them the truth.

STUFF TO TALK ABOUT:

- Discussions about normal, healthy bodily functions should be relaxed and without judgment. Yes, teaching privacy when talking about certain issues is important, but you don't want to do it in such a way that your children feel ashamed to poo, fart, or have a runny tummy. The same goes for sex. Talking about it must be a normal part of education and should be done as easily and with the same facial expressions as if you are spreading butter on toast!

RECOMMENDED RESOURCES:

- Two great books that I definitely recommend are *Bringing Up Girls* and *Bringing Up Boys*, both by Dr. James Dobson, the well-known American family expert.
- A very insightful book on how the sexes operate differently is *Love & Respect* by Dr. Emerson Eggerichs.

SCRIPTURES:

Genesis 1:27–28 So God created mankind in His own image, in the image of God He created them; male and female He created them. God blessed them and said to them, "Be fruitful and increase in number; fill the earth and subdue it. Rule over the fish in the sea and the birds in the sky and over every living creature that moves on the ground."

Genesis 2:18 The Lord God said, "It is not good for the man to be alone. I will make a helper suitable for him."

Genesis 2:24–25 That is why a man leaves his father and mother and is united to his wife, and they become one flesh. Adam and his wife were both naked, and they felt no shame.

Psalm 139:13 For You created my inmost being; You knit me together in my mother's womb.

Proverbs 5:15–19 Drink water from your own cistern, running water from your own well. Should your springs overflow in the streets, your streams of water in the public squares? Let them be yours alone, never to be shared with strangers. May your fountain be blessed, and may you rejoice in the wife of your youth. A loving doe, a graceful deer— may her breasts satisfy you always, may you ever be intoxicated with her love.

Ecclesiastes 9:9 Enjoy life with your wife, whom you love, all the days of this meaningless life that God has given you under the sun—all your meaningless days. For this is your lot in life and in your toilsome labor under the sun.

Song of Songs 1:2 Let him kiss me with the kisses of his mouth—for your love is more delightful than wine.

Song of Songs 4:10 How delightful is your love, my sister, my bride! How much more pleasing is your love than wine, and the fragrance of your perfume more than any spice!

Song of Songs 7:6–12 How beautiful you are and how pleasing, my love, with your delights! Your stature is like that of the palm, and your breasts like clusters of fruit. I said, "I will climb the palm tree; I will take hold of its fruit." May your breasts be like clusters of grapes on the vine, the fragrance of your breath like apples, and your mouth like the best wine. **She:** May the wine go straight to my beloved, flowing gently over lips and teeth. I belong to my beloved, and his desire is for me. Come, my beloved, let us go to the countryside, let us spend the night in the villages. Let us go early to the vineyards to see if the vines have budded, if their blossoms have opened, and if the pomegranates are in bloom— there I will give you my love.

1 Corinthians 7:3–5 The husband should fulfill his marital duty to his wife, and likewise the wife to her husband. The wife does not have authority over her own body but yields it to her husband. In the same way, the husband does not have authority over his own body but yields it to his wife. Do not deprive each other except perhaps by mutual consent and for a time, so that you may devote yourselves to prayer. Then come together again so that Satan will not tempt you because of your lack of self-control.

Ephesians 2:10 For we are God's handiwork, created in Christ Jesus to do good works, which God prepared in advance for us to do.

Hebrews 13:4 Marriage should be honored by all, and the marriage bed kept pure, for God will judge the adulterer and all the sexually immoral.

CHAPTER 5

HOW TO HANDLE THOSE UNCOMFORTABLE QUESTIONS—LIKE A BOSS

The following examples are guidelines on how to implement the 7 P's. With this approach you will be able to point your children in the right direction and show them God's truth without sounding judgmental or negative.

Examples 1–4: Before the age of seven, keep your discussions basic and don't give too much detail.

Examples 5–9: When your children reach the age of seven, it is time to start telling them what sex is, because they will hear about it at school. This is also the time to warn them that some of their friends might want to show them inappropriate pictures or have inappropriate discussions. You have to start preparing them for such scenarios. Practice it, be prepared, and regularly initiate these discussions with your children.

Examples 10–12: When your child is nine years or older (some children are ready before others, girls are usually ready before boys) it is a good time to discuss the more difficult concepts, like homosexuality. By this age, a strong foundation should have been laid, so that you can discuss the trickier questions. I wish I could include all the questions children have when it comes to sexuality, but then I will never finish writing! The ones I have included, are the most common and with a little bit of creative adjustment, you will be able to formulate very good and practical answers for all their questions, by applying the 7 P's.

Discussion examples

1. "Mommy, why do I look different from my brother?"

"God made women and men different, and their bodies differ. You look different from your brother because he is a boy, and you are a girl! God gave your brother a penis and He gave you a vagina. Isn't it wonderful that God made you and your brother different? Sometimes you like different things, isn't it? And remember, even though you look different, God loves you both equally." (Positive + Parent)

2. "Where did I come from?"

"You grew in my body. All mothers have a special place where babies grow. It is called the womb or the uterus." (Show them a simple picture of the womb and where it is located.) *"You grew in my womb, very close to my heart. Feel here… Can you hear how my heart is beating? I was so excited to have you! Then, when you were strong and big enough, you came out of my body. That is why we celebrate your birthday!" (Positive + Parent)*

3. "How did I get out of your body?"

Vaginal birth: *"When you were big and strong enough, I packed my bags and your baby clothes, and we went to the hospital. Mommies have a special opening between their legs, called the vagina, where the baby comes out. When the time was right, the doctor and the nurses helped me to softly push and push until your head came out. Then the rest of your body came out. It was such an awesome moment when I held you in my arms for the first time! I cried a big, long happy cry!"*

Caesarean section: *"Sometimes, the doctor decides that it would be best to rather make a small cut right here to get the baby out."* (Show them your scar or a simple picture.) *Then the doctor closes the cut with stitches. Don't worry, they gave me special medicine, so I didn't feel any pain. To hold you in my arms for the first time was the most wonderful feeling in the whole wide world! Wow, what a special way to come into the world! Come, let's go look in the mirror. Who do you think you look like? I think you got my nose!"* (Also explain a vaginal birth to them.)

Tell them things about their birth and what a special time it was. Tell them about your pregnancy, how they kicked you in the ribs, or how you could feel their hiccups. Tell them that you couldn't wait to meet them and how God wove them together in the special secret place that was their home for nine months. Tell them how excited God was to make them and that He has a big plan for them! God made marriage and family. It was His great idea. (Positive + Parent)

4. "How does the baby get inside the mommy's body?"

"Mommies have tiny eggs in their bodies. Daddies make seeds in their bodies. When one of the seeds meets up with the mommy's egg, it melts together and grows into a baby. It takes a mommy and a daddy to make a baby." (Partner)

5. "How does the seed get into the mommy's body?"

"Do you remember when we went to auntie Katy's wedding? You were one of the little bridesmaids! Do you remember the table full of presents? Auntie Katie and her husband could only open those presents on their wedding day. Now, just like

that, God has a special gift for newly married couples which they can open on their wedding day. It is called sex." (Present)

"God says that only people who are married to one another should open this gift. It is like a glue that keeps them together and it is God's way of making families strong. This gift is also God's way of showing us how close He wants to be with us." (Protection + Provision)

"Because the man and woman are married, their bodies now belong to one another. When a husband and wife are alone, they can hold one another, love one another, and hug and kiss and lie close together. The husband can fit his penis into his wife's vagina. God made our bodies to fit together perfectly, like a puzzle! That is called sex. It makes them feel good and helps them to love one another in a very special way. The daddy's seeds are also called sperm. The seed is tiny and has a wiggly tail that makes sure that it gets to the mommy's egg quickly. The seeds have a race to see who will get to the egg first! The winner gets to melt together with the egg. This is the way babies are made." (Positive + Parent)

"Someday, when you are married, you and your husband can also open your special wedding present from God! How exciting!" (Provision + Present)

"But remember, sex is not right if you do it when you are not married. It is like your special toys that you don't really want to share with others… Sex is like that. It should not be shared with anyone except your husband or wife. To share it with other people would spoil the present. It is also private, so if you have any questions about sex, you can ask me any time. It is safe to talk about sex at our house. Don't talk about it at school. If anyone else is talking about sex, I want you to walk away and tell me about it. I love talking to you about these things. Will you let me know if you have more questions?" (Private + Protection)

If you are a parent who struggled to fall pregnant and needed medical help, or if you had a miscarriage, you could explain it to your child in the following way (this is a very simple explanation, so feel free to add more detail for older children):

"Sometimes, a mommy and daddy might struggle to fall pregnant. It can be for various reasons—maybe there is a problem with the daddy's seeds, or there is a problem in the mommy's uterus. That is when they call in the help of special doctors. These doctors specialize in helping parents to have a baby. At other times, the mommy can fall pregnant, but the tiny baby stops growing. When a baby dies inside the mommy's body, we call that a miscarriage. A mommy must go to the hospital when that happens so that the doctors can help her. These parents feel very sad and might be sad for a long time. They might want another baby and may also need the help of special doctors. There are many different ways that they can assist the mommy and daddy, and sometimes it can take a long time. But isn't it amazing that God provided a way for parents that struggle, so that they can have a baby!" (Positive + Provision)

"The reality is, there are some people that really want to have a baby but can't. They try medical intervention, but it doesn't work. These married couples might be very sad and even angry with God. It is a very heartsore situation. Just know, that even if that is the case, God holds them in His hands. We do not know the reasons, but we can trust that God knows best and that He has a special place in His heart for people that suffer. Many times, these people then decide to adopt a child. Adoption is when someone takes care of a child whose parents aren't around anymore. It's a wonderful way for them to get the chance to be parents, as well as giving a child a home." (Parent + Positive + Provision)

Try to identify the 7 P's yourself from here on:

6. "What is a condom?"

First ask, *"Where did you hear about or see a condom?"*

"A condom stops a woman from becoming pregnant. It keeps back the seeds from the daddy so that it doesn't touch the mommy's egg. It is almost like a little bag that catches the seeds before it can swim to the egg! Sometimes parents decide to

wait for a specific time to have a baby and then they need a condom to make sure that they don't get pregnant before the right time."

7. "What are those soft, white sticker things you keep in the bathroom cupboard, Mommy?"

"Those are called pads. They are made to fit into my underwear to protect it from a little bit of fluid that will come out of my vagina once a month. God created a woman's body so special! It cleans itself from the inside! When a girl reaches a certain age, the part of her body where the baby will grow starts to clean itself. The pads help us to not make a mess in our underwear and it keeps us dry and clean. Isn't that clever?!"

You can also explain how a tampon works: *"These are called tampons. They are designed to easily fit into a woman's vagina. Do you see this string? It helps the woman to pull it out again when it is full and needs to be changed. Tampons also absorb all the fluid so that it doesn't mess up her underwear. Do you remember when you bumped your nose and it started bleeding? We put a piece of cotton wool in your nose so that the blood didn't make a mess everywhere. A tampon works in the same way!"*

This is an easy way to explain pads and tampons to a small child who has a lot of questions. At age nine, when you explain menstruation, you can go into more detail. (See *Chapter 6: Prepare Them for Puberty*.)

8. "What is AIDS?"

"AIDS is the name of a disease and anyone can get it if they don't look after their bodies. When you have measles, mumps, chicken pox or a cold, everyone can see that you are sick, because you have a runny nose or spots all over your body! But with AIDS, we cannot see that the person is sick for a long time, because the virus

hides in the person's blood. You cannot get AIDS through the air like a cold. You can only get it if the blood or bodily fluids of someone who has AIDS touches your blood or bodily fluids. So, touching someone's blood without gloves on your hands is not a good idea!" (When your children reach puberty, you can explain how AIDS can be transferred through semen or bodily fluids.) *"So, if your friend hurt him- or herself, never touch his or her blood and rather take your friend to a teacher. We never know whether people have AIDS. But even if we do, it cannot just rub off on you, so you can still give them hugs, sit next to them, and play with them.*

"Remember, our private parts are private. That means that it is just for you. We don't touch someone else's blood or private parts. Just know that you don't have to be scared, because God always protects us."

(You can also explain the difference between HIV and AIDS when the time is right.)

9. Discussion about sexual games

"God loves us so much and He gave us our bodies as an amazingly special gift. I understand why you are interested in other people's bodies and why they are interested in yours. We all know that these parts are special, and we want to know more about special things. It's almost like opening your presents before Christmas. Before Christmas Day, you can't wait to open your presents, so it's okay and completely natural to be inquisitive. It's also natural to want to know more about special things. It makes us feel grown-up.

"But because your body is special—a gift—it is meant to be private. God created your private parts for a special purpose and not as toys for other children to play with. Even though it is okay to be inquisitive, I don't want you to show your private parts to other children. And I don't want you to ask to see theirs. If you keep your body and your private parts special and private, it will help you to

always feel that God made you in a special way. And God wants you to keep your body for the special person you will marry one day. He wants to care for you and keep you from getting hurt in any way. If any child or grown-up asks to see your private parts or shows you theirs, you must say NO in a loud voice and tell someone on your helping hand.

"I'll tell you what; a good game to play instead is [insert favorite game that you know they love to play with their friends]. *Let's go see if we can find the props you need."*

10. Questions about the LGBTQ+ (lesbian, gay, bisexual, transsexual, queer, etc.) lifestyle—even if your child doesn't ask these questions, it would be wise for you to initiate this conversation at the appropriate age, because they will come across certain terms in school

Doctors and scientists disagree about many things with regard to LBGTQ+, and we as Christians even disagree with one another. If the answers were so obvious, we would know how to explain it to our children. Because sexuality is very complicated in general, and there are many different theories out there, it confuses us even more. I don't have the answers either, but I do know what the Bible teaches us. So let's use God's wisdom to answer our children's questions. (For a more detailed discussion, see *Chapter 10: Teach Them About Healthy Relationships.*)

First of all, before you talk about LGBTQ+, make sure the foundation has been laid about God's original plan for marriage, what sex is, and where it all belongs. With a firm foundation in God's life-giving ways, it will be easier to explain the more difficult concepts. We must make sure that we always guide our children's identity—who they are, and how God made them—towards Christ. If our identity is based in Jesus and we believe what He says about us, we are on our way to real freedom.

Secondly, remember the 7 P's, especially when answering these types of questions. Let LOVE be your guide and kindness your ally. Yes, God did make us male and female, and He did say that it is good. And yes, God's original plan is the best and will always be. But sin entered the world and from that day, everything started to rot—even us. As Christians living in a world that isn't going to last, with hearts full of sin and bodies that will eventually die, we only have one chance to love one another the way Jesus did. Teach your children what God says about marriage, sex, and sexuality. Also teach them *why* God says these things. But most of all, *show* them how Jesus treated the woman at the well, the tax collector, the prostitute, Judas, and me and you in our worst sinful states—with grace, love, and kindness. Teach them to show love to their (LBGTQ+) neighbors, no matter what. Also keep the parents of the LBGTQ+ person in mind. Often, they are the ones who especially need support, love, and acceptance. The pain some of those parents experience can be excruciating, especially if their children (or they, themselves) are rejected by friends and family.

Another thing to highlight is that sometimes, when a boy wants to play with dolls and dress in their sister's Frozen outfit or take dance lessons, or tomboy girls don't want to wear dresses and rather want to play rugby, it doesn't always mean that they are struggling with their sexual identity or that they are transgender or homosexual. Most often it is just a natural developmental phase that kids go through. However, if you have any concerns as a parent, I recommend you and your child have open and honest discussions about their feelings. Love and accept them as they are, but always lovingly point them in God's life-giving way. Make an appointment with a qualified person who can assist you and your family in this area. It may be that there are past deep hurts that need to be dealt with.

Here is an example of how you can explain some of these concepts to children aged 9–12 (you can add more details when they are ready to understand):

"Sometimes a man will choose to love another man in the special way that mommy and daddy love one another. That is called being homosexual, gay (male) or

lesbian (female). Many people choose to rather love, and even marry, someone of the same gender, and we should respect that, even if we disagree (1 Peter 2:17, Matthew 7:12, James 2:9).

"Sometimes a boy will want to wear girls' clothes; maybe even play sports that we think are girls' sports or play with girls' toys. And there is nothing wrong with that. Sometimes you also want to do what your brother (or sister) is doing. That is how we discover what we like and where we fit in. But there are times that some boys will want to carry on wearing girl clothes as an adult or dress up and wear make-up like a woman. I don't understand all the reasons why they feel that way. But I do know that God loves them just as much as He loves you. God's heart is for us to love that person, too, just like we love our other friends. We should treat them with the same love and respect we treat our best friends.

"But do you remember when I explained to you that God had made a man and a woman, male and female, in His image? He said that we must be fruitful and make babies and fill the earth! He also said that a man will be joined to his wife and they will become one flesh. Well, marriage and children are His idea and His original plan. God's plan for our lives, as well as His rules, are like an umbrella protecting us from the rain, hail and lightning—the consequences that can come our way if we make choices that don't honor God.

"But sometimes people choose not to follow God's way—they move away from His umbrella—for many different reasons. Even as Christians we sometimes do that. God still loves us very much, but now we are left vulnerable. God gave us free will, and His biggest desire is for us to choose Him and stay under His umbrella. Sadly, people sometimes choose not to follow His ways. We will not always understand the reasons or the circumstances that make people choose differently. Many of those people struggle to be accepted and are treated unkindly. We should always show love to them, even if we disagree. God's biggest rule is this: Love God and love your neighbor as yourself. It is as simple as that. Never be unkind to people who are different from you or make different choices. That hurts God's heart very much. God loves all His Creation, and He wants us to show love to *our neighbors, no matter what they believe. And for us to really love our neighbors, we need to get to know them. That means spending time with them and inviting them to a party, too! How would you feel if you were to be excluded just because you believe in or choose different things? It is a choice to love someone, especially if they are different from us or believe different things. God expects us to treat ALL people with love and respect. If we don't, we are in the wrong.*

"If you have more questions about this, come to me so that we can work through it together."

11. Inappropriate scenes on the television

The other day, I stumbled upon a movie with an age restriction of nine years, and I was shocked. Not only does one of the characters—a very kind homosexual man—convince a lady of 39 years old to have his baby (by insemination), but it also showed a five-second sex scene with this same lady and another married man (with whom she was in an adulterous relationship). The scene was complete with sound effects, facial expressions, and vigorous movements under the sheets. I don't know about you, but that is not what I want my children to see as the norm. If my daughter was to regularly see movies such as that, no matter her age, with no discussion about what is happening in it, what do you think will happen in her brain and her heart? Do you think that she might conclude that what she saw is okay, normal and acceptable; that it's how it should be? Yes, talking about uncomfortable things puts you out of your comfort zone, but if you don't talk about it, you are leaving it up to the world to teach your children about sexuality. Your once-off talk about 'what goes where' and 'wait until you are married' is not going to cut it.

Imagine that you and your child are watching a movie together and an inappropriate scene is shown on the screen. How do you handle the situation? Turning off the television and ignoring what both of you saw is only going to raise more questions or confirm whatever your child had already started to think. And because you are not addressing the situation, your child will assume that you are not open to discuss it or, even worse, that what they saw is acceptable. With no discussion, you lose your chance to change or rectify any wrong thinking and assumptions. Having a discussion is vital and should, of course, be tailored to your child's age. Below is an example of how I would approach this subject with my 9-year-old if we should stumble upon an inappropriate movie scene. (Note that at this age my daughter does already know where babies come from.)

"Let's talk about what we just saw on TV. You know how God feels about families. Families are so close to His heart, and that is why He made certain rules to protect us from pain, hurt and rejection. And as you also know, people sometimes choose not to follow God's rules. Instead, they follow their own desires, wants and needs, and they decide for themselves what is important. You just saw an unmarried lady (let's call her Angelina) with a married man (let's call him Brad), in the same bed. Not only is she not married to him, but she is also in bed with a man who is married to another woman (let's call her Jennifer). How do you think Jennifer will feel if she finds out that her husband, Brad, is sharing his body and his sexuality, the gift God gave to him and his wife, with someone else? Her heart will be broken! Jennifer will feel so much pain in her heart and might never, ever trust a man again. That will make God so sad. The unmarried lady, Angelina, also chose not to listen to God's rules, and her heart can also get hurt because this man, Brad, might not want to be with her forever. And what about Brad? He might think that he is having a good time, but when these women find out about each other, or if he gets bored, he will become less likely to stick to one woman and he will lose both of them. In the process, so many people will feel alone, hurt, sad, guilty, rejected, and shameful. That is not what God wants for us or for families!

"When a baby is born, that baby didn't ask to be here. A baby deserves a mommy and a daddy who is always there for him or her, and who will always love and care for him or her. That is the best way and it's God's original plan. If we choose

to leave our husband or wife for someone else, or hurt our husband or wife's trust, we hurt our children's hearts as well.

"This is why I don't want you to watch movies with an age restriction, or any movie without first asking me if it is okay to watch. Sometimes there will be scenes in movies that go against what we teach you and we do not want you to think that what you see in those movies is God's way. He has a different way; His ways are not the same as the world's ways. God's way is best.

"Also, sometimes when we see people kissing passionately or lying in bed together, it can give us sexual feelings, which are feelings that make us feel good in our private parts. Having sexual feelings isn't wrong, it is healthy and normal, but it belongs within marriage. We are not supposed to look at people who are in bed together. Watching people having sex or doing sexual acts is called pornography. Pornography is very dangerous. Remember, sex is private and not for anyone else to see, only for our marriage partner. That is why it is dangerous to watch people having sex. It can give us such strong sexual feelings that we might want to act on. It makes us desire to have sex before we are married. Those feelings can be very powerful, and make us weak and give in. God gave us sexual feelings because they are good, healthy, normal, and wonderful to share with your husband or wife only. It is His special wedding present to a married couple. It is so worth waiting for! So if you are watching a movie and you see people having sex, I want you to be strong and turn it off or walk away. Come and tell me about it so that we can discuss what you saw and you know how to handle it if it should happen again."

12. Discussions about masturbation and pornography

Masturbation is probably one of the most uncomfortable topics to discuss with your offspring, and where most parents need a bit of a hand.

The good news is that it is possible to have discussions about it without that awkward, uncomfortable, earth-please-swallow-me mini panic attacks we all get sometimes. Paving the way to these discussions when they are still little will assist you big time if you accidentally walk in on something you wish you had a delete button for.

First of all, there is nothing wrong with your child. Secondly, our bodies were designed by God to feel good when touched in certain places. Our job as parents is just to help our kids to recognize healthy boundaries when it comes to this form of touching while they are young.

Ages 3–4

Kids in this age group are still learning how to behave in public, so handle the touching of private parts the same way you will handle it if they pick their noses in public. At this age, kids seldom imagine anything sexual when they touch their private parts. They are just enjoying a new sensation. In a gentle manner and a soft voice, explain that just like we don't pick our noses, we also don't touch ourselves there, except when we are cleaning ourselves or when getting checked by a doctor.

Ages 5–8

This is a good time to start talking about masturbation, as kids are more likely to talk openly. And it is so important to start laying a solid foundation. These early conversations don't have to be descriptive, but it shouldn't be so vague that they don't know what is being discussed. Talking about masturbation in a natural tone of voice and explaining in simple terms how certain parts of the body feel good when touched can help parents pave the way for open and honest conversations later on.

Boundaries for this type of touching should be discussed as well. Kids have no context of what these feelings are about, so it is important to discuss it openly so that there is no room for confusion. Because masturbation is a topic that is discussed at school, it is very likely that your children will hear about it during this phase. And they will probably be misinformed if that is the only input they receive about it. Now is the time to guide their views and connect masturbation to its sexual nature, with marriage. This pleasure-touch should rather be associated with and saved for a special part of marriage. If you choose not to discuss this topic, it can result in masturbation without any boundaries as they grow up.

Remember: no condemning messages. Horrified looks, tears, and yelling are all ways of shaming them. Punishing them for masturbating is also a form of shaming. Shaming might stop the behavior, but it won't turn them into healthy adults. If you think that your child's behavior regarding this is outside of normal frequency, it might be a form of self-soothing behavior. A good idea then, is to ask them a few questions, such as, "Do you feel lonely, sad or afraid?" Excessive masturbation is usually a symptom of something else, such as a deeper emotional need. Playing with them, getting them to exercise, providing intellectual stimulation and giving them extra quality time and hugs on a regular basis might solve the problem. If excessive masturbation is coupled with other behavioral problems or obsessive-compulsive behavior, you will need to seek professional help.

Ages 8–12

By now, kids are more aware of the existence of masturbation, as well as pornography. It is very important that parents continue giving their children a context for what they see and hear at school or in the media. At the age of 11 is a good time to sit them down and go into a bit more detail with this discussion. Always refer back to God's original plan for sex, where sexual pleasure should be associated with marriage. That is God's design. The goal isn't to stop the behavior, but to shape the person your child is becoming. If you don't talk about God's design for their sexuality, your kids may not understand why you are telling them to save sexual pleasure for marriage. Without an understanding of God's original plan for sex, sexual behavior will become a rule, and guess what…? Kids break rules. Getting them to understand this means talking about uncomfortable topics often. Kids easily pick up when parents are uncomfortable, and then they can make wrong associations, for example that sexual feelings are wrong, or they experience guilt or shame about it. I suggest that if you are really very uncomfortable, you make a coffee date with your spouse, or your best friend, and practice the conversation with one another first.

You might get some very embarrassed looks or long, awkward silences. That's okay! Push through. If you are silent, the only voice they will hear will be the voice of the world.

This is also the age at which many kids get exposed to pornography. And you will have to handle it. If you are under the impression that your child is watching porn, sit them down and talk to them about it. Yes, they might feel embarrassed, but how you are going to handle the situation will be vital. You want them to still be able to approach you in the future, so don't mess this one up!

Remember to include the 7 P's in your discussion. There should be no judgment or condemnation in your tone of voice. In fact, if you have messed up concerning pornography, now is a good time to be honest, to man up and tell them about your own struggles.

Here are a few tips you can keep in mind:

- Remember the 7 P's.
- Remember that sexual feelings/arousal is normal and healthy. But it has to be put in the right context—marriage.
- Share your own struggles with pornography if you feel comfortable. If you do this, it will help to open the communication lines and make them feel less ashamed and embarrassed.
- Talk about the consequences and dangers of pornography.

- Talk about what God says about sex and sexuality, where it belongs, and why (see *Chapter 8: Teach Them the Big Deal About Sex*).
- Do not overreact, punish, condemn, or shame.
- Talk about pornography often and offer to be an accountability partner. Put strategies in place so that your children don't have access to it on the computer and make sure to have parental controls on their electronic devices (tablets, phones, and the like).
- Also talk about trust and the fact that you are there for them if this is something they want to talk about. You can explain that we all make mistakes, and when we bring it to the table, and to God, we can deal with it in the correct way.

LET'S GET PRACTICAL

STUFF TO DO:

- If there are any other questions you can think of which are not covered in this section, I suggest you write out your own answer and include the 7 P's as a guideline. Rather be prepared for those unexpected questions so that you can answer confidently and truthfully with love, positivity, and a non-judgmental attitude. You can email it to me so I can assist you if you struggle. My details are in the back of the book.
- Remember, always point them towards God's original plan for marriage and for our sexuality.
- Start collecting age-appropriate images, diagrams, and YouTube videos that can explain certain details. Keep it in a special file on your computer, ready to aid you in your discussions. You do not want them to accidentally stumble upon things such as your home birth video, for example, before preparing them for what they are about to see!

STUFF TO TALK ABOUT:

- Practice answering tough questions by using the 7 P's as a guideline. Don't get too stressed about it. As you can see, every answer does not have to cover all of the 7 P's. You can also answer in a way that is more comfortable for you or leave out certain details if you feel that it's a bit too early for your child to learn about it. Just stick to God's truth and initiate conversations as often as possible. And remember to not just discuss God's word, but also God's actions…Jesus was respectful, loving and kind ALL THE TIME, to EVERYBODY.

- The LGBTQ+ lifestyle is a sensitive and controversial subject, but don't shy away from teaching your children God's truth—starting with the basics and building on it from there. Do it with love and lead by example.

RECOMMENDED RESOURCES:

- *The Wonderful Way that Babies are Made*, by Larry Christenson
- *The Miracle of Creation* series, by Susan Horner
- *What is God's Design for My Body?* by Susan Horner
- *Beautifully Made!* series, by Julie Hiramine

SCRIPTURES:

Psalm 139:13–16 For you created my inmost being; you knit me together in my mother's womb. I praise you because I am fearfully and wonderfully made; your works are wonderful, I know that full well. My frame was not hidden from you when I was made in the secret place, when I was woven together in the depths of the earth. Your eyes saw my unformed body; all the days ordained for me were written in your book before one of them came to be.

Matthew 7:12 So in everything, do to others what you would have them do to you, for this sums up the Law and the Prophets.

James 2:9 But if you show favoritism, you sin and are convicted by the law as lawbreakers.

1 Peter 2:17 Show proper respect to everyone, love the family of believers, fear God, honor the emperor.

Chapter 6

Prepare Them for Puberty—Before It Hits

What an exciting phase! Your child is bursting with hormones and you, as parents, are bursting with conflicting emotions and, depending on your age, the *lack* of hormones! I, for instance, will be in the throes of menopause when my daughters turn 16 years old. I'm sure it's going to be a very interesting time for my husband!

So, to make sure that we remain a loving family, preparation is key. Just as my family and I need to know what to expect when menopause hits—or any other big change we can foresee—my kids also need to know what to expect when puberty hits. The more understanding there is, the more grace there will be. That includes all members of the household, for instance in our case my husband is the only male in the house and will need to be on top of his game in the approaching hormone-filled (and lack thereof) time.

Our bodies were designed to go through changes. God made it that way. However, we are not just physical beings; we are sexual, emotional, mental, social and, most of all, spiritual beings as well. Changes will take place in these areas, too, and it needs to be handled with wisdom, love, and acceptance. Teaching our children about their bodies is not going to involve only basic biology. Character building and values must also be included.

A good time to start explaining these changes will be when your child is about nine years old. You will notice that they have fewer questions as they get older. Some reasons for this might be that they get their information from other sources, or their questions might trigger a too sensitive topic in your house if your reactions to previous questions had not been what they had wanted or needed it to be. Your job is to always keep the communication lines open. Kids *do* want to know, so always initiate conversation, even if they roll their eyes at you.

This chapter is an example of *how* to approach certain discussion points in the area of puberty, as well as what needs to be taught during this phase. Because the *how* is the main point, I'm not going to include all the changes and details that puberty entails. That can fill a book by itself! In the end, you want to give your children the correct information in a positive and loving way, without making them feel guilty or shameful about their amazing bodies. When your children ask you questions that are unexpected or outside your comfort zone, take a deep breath, ask God what to say, do your research, and get back to them with the answer at an appropriate time. Your answer should always include not just the correct information, but also the *why*. If children understand the *why*, they are better informed and equipped to make better choices regarding their sexuality.

Remember to include the 7 P's while you have these discussions with your children.

1. Teach them about the seen and unseen changes in both boys and girls

This is very important, as it brings understanding to the needs and development of the opposite sex. It can also give you an opportunity to explain that making fun of someone else while they are going through these changes can be hurtful and humiliating for that person, because puberty is a sensitive and emotional time. It is an opportunity to teach your children respect for the opposite sex. The following is an example of how to include the 7 P's in your discussion, and it will assist you in pointing your children towards God's purpose for sexuality and His wonderful design for our bodies.

"How do our bodies know when to start changing?"

"Good question! God made our bodies very special and also very unique. We all start changing at different times, anywhere between eight and 13 years of age. Sometimes it starts even later! In our brains we have a little gland called the pituitary gland. It is as small as a pea and it produces a special hormone that tells our reproductive organs to start producing certain hormones. These hormones trigger the changes in our bodies. It's like a traffic light that suddenly turns green. The cars start driving when the light turns green. The pituitary gland is like the traffic light that turns green, and then our hormones are ready to move, like the cars, and they cause our bodies to change. This happens slowly and not all at once. Thank goodness for that! Imagine waking up one morning and looking like a fully-grown man or woman! I would freak out! God sure knew what He was doing when He designed our bodies!"

"But what are REPRODUCTIVE ORGANS?"

"Reproductive organs are special organs in our bodies that have a very special function… to make babies! We can reproduce. Boys and girls have different reproductive organs. A boy has a penis, testicles, a scrotum, and a prostate gland. A girl has a vagina, clitoris, and labia—which together is called the vulva, a uterus, and ovaries." (Show a simple medical diagram, a simple line drawing of both gender's reproductive organs with all the different parts and medical names indicated. You can even discuss the current slang for these private bits, but teach them the correct medical terms, as well as the appropriate use of nicknames. Certain words are simply vulgar, disrespectful, and not in good taste.)

"A man's testicles make millions of tiny little seeds every day. These seeds are super tiny. In fact, it is the smallest cell in the human body! That is why you cannot see it with your naked eye—you need a strong microscope. These little seeds each have their own little tail, like a tadpole! It helps them to swim to the woman's egg.

"A woman has tiny little eggs. And guess what? An egg cell is the biggest cell in the human body, but it is still too small to see with the naked eye. Little girls are born with all the egg cells they will ever have! When they reach a certain age, one ripe egg cell gets released from her ovaries to travel to her uterus every month. The uterus is a special and safe place where babies grow.

"Our reproductive organs keep the seeds (sperm) and the eggs safe for the exact right time. A woman's reproductive organs are also specially designed so that a baby can grow in her body. A man cannot carry a baby in his body. God made men a bit stronger so that they can protect the mommy and the baby. Daddies have a very important job! That is why, when little boys grow up and they reach a certain age, their pituitary gland releases a hormone called testosterone. The boy will become taller with broader shoulders, stronger muscles, a deep voice and body hair, particularly on his face, chest, and private parts. Boys can also feel tender in the breast area and may have some swelling there, but don't worry, the swelling and hardness will go away, it won't grow into breasts!

"Girls also go through changes. Their breasts grow bigger, so this is a good time for them to start wearing a bra so that their breasts are supported, feel more comfortable and don't show through their clothes. Girls' hips become rounder, and they start menstruating. They also grow hair on their bodies, particularly their private parts, as well as under their arms. Some boys' and girls' skin gets very oily and that can cause pimples. Pimples are small red spots or bumps on your face, back, or neck. If you fiddle with it, it can get worse, so if you get a pimple, come show me and I will teach you how to take care of it."

"MENSTRUATION? What is that?"

"A woman's body is designed to carry a baby. God made our bodies so wonderfully and also so different! When a girl reaches a certain age (and that age is different for every girl), her pituitary gland releases a hormone called estrogen. Estrogen is the cause of all her bodily changes. Every month, a little layer that looks like blood builds up in her uterus, and one of her eggs is released from her ovaries and travels to the uterus. This is called ovulation." (Use your line drawing to show them where this happens.) *"If that egg doesn't meet up with a seed from the daddy, this tiny egg and the layer of blood must come out through the vagina. This is called menstruation, and girls need special protection in their underwear to prevent a mess. They can use pads or tampons for that."* (Show them what it looks like and how it works.) *"Girls can be a bit uncomfortable during this time of the month, and they sometimes feel extra emotional or moody as well. In the beginning, a girl's cycle can be irregular, but as she gets older, it will become more regular—about every 28 to 30 days. A girl can keep track of her periods on a calendar so that she can know when her next one will start, and she can then be prepared. A period is another name for menstruation. This bleeding, which is altogether about half a cup, lasts about three to five days and happens to every woman, until about the age of 50. She then stops menstruating. When girls are menstruating, they must take care of themselves and pay extra attention to hygiene. Boys must also start paying more attention to hygiene when they reach this age, as both boys' and girls' sweat glands start working harder. And it's not fun for anyone having smelly kids around, is it? Girls can still do their favorite activities, like sports, dancing or even swimming during menstruation! It's very good for a girl to keep exercising while she has her period."*

"And boys? Do they menstruate?"

"No, they don't. They have completely different reproductive organs, remember? Girls are born with all their eggs already in their bodies, and it grows with them until they are old enough and one egg gets released every month. Boys' testicles make millions of tiny seeds every day! We call them sperm. The prostate also makes a special liquid called semen, in which these tiny seeds can swim. Sometimes boys' bodies want to get rid of excess sperm. This usually happens at night when they sleep.

We call it a wet dream or a nocturnal emission. The boy's penis will get hard and semen flows out. It can be a bit messy, but he can change his underwear and mom or dad can quickly put it in the wash. It is normal and shows that a boy is starting to grow up. Boys' penises also sometimes get hard and grow bigger without them having control over it, sometimes without any reason. This is also normal. The best way to handle this is to think of something else, like homework or a favorite sport. When a boy's penis gets hard, it is called an erection, but there are lots of other different names for it. (Here you can name a few slang names for an erection, for example, a hard-on, a stiffy, or a boner. Expect a lot of giggles!)

"Boys are sometimes worried about their penis size. Boys, the size of your penis doesn't matter. Your body is perfectly made and is just right. Your penis is also growing and will only be fully grown when you are an adult. Likewise, girls are sometimes worried about their bodies as well. All girls have different shapes and breast sizes. Girls, your bodies are beautiful, feminine, and just right. God made it perfectly. Look after your body, eat healthily, exercise, and accept your body. You only have one body for your whole life, and it's God's house; He wants to live in it. We have a responsibility to take care of our beautiful bodies."

2. Teach them about sexual feelings, sexual intercourse, pregnancy and birth

"One of the reasons that we have to make good and healthy choices is because our bodies are ready to make babies very early on in our lives. Even though our bodies are ready, it doesn't mean that we are ready. We are not just a body, remember? We are also social, mental, emotional, and spiritual beings. Our emotional and mental side takes much longer to develop, and we have to be careful not to just follow our physical desires, as this can cause a lot of trouble for us. We have to practice self-control—a very important life skill! Our bodies are meant to be private—that means that it is just for you. And God wants us to only share our bodies with the person we are married to. That is the safest place, both for us and for a baby that can come into this world."

"Yes! You told us that God gave married couples a special gift… sex!"

"Yes, He did! I think it is a very clever and very special gift! But it's not always easy to wait for this special present, because our bodies have sexual feelings before we get married. It's almost like knowing what you are going to get for your birthday, but you are not allowed to unwrap it before the big day. You cannot wait to open it and play with your new toy! It is the same with sex. It is normal to be curious and have these sexual feelings while you grow up. It shows that you are healthy, and God wants to teach you that He is the one who gives you these feelings. But that is why we must practice self-control and remember why God made sex. By delaying sexual gratification and release, God is not limiting our joy but rather increasing it. He doesn't want us to have bad memories of our sexual experiences. Sex is a special gift that bonds a man and a woman together, like superglue! If we 'glue' ourselves to just anyone, or to more than one person, we are just going to mess ourselves up. It must be so painful to continuously tear yourself loose from one person and then 'glue' yourself to the next person! In doing that, you leave pieces of yourself everywhere. God doesn't want that for us. Sex is the glue that sticks you to your spouse forever! That is why He made sex: so that you can experience a different type of intimacy with your spouse, someone you made a promise to and who made a promise to you. You don't have this intimacy with anyone else. The promise you make on your wedding day (the most important pinky-promise you will EVER make) is a lifelong commitment that you make, a promise to take care of another person. God takes this pinky-promise very seriously. That is what makes it different from any other relationship in our lives. Sex is a celebration of that promise—something to enjoy passionately as a married couple. This is also the way babies are made. So it is important to wait for this present from God. You have to wait—for your own good, for the good of your spouse and for the good of a baby that might come into this world from this special union. Sexual intercourse will be waiting for you, ready to be enjoyed at the proper time."

"Sexual what?"

"Sexual intercourse; it's another word for sex. That is when a man puts his penis in the woman's vagina.

"First, the penis gets harder and bigger. Do you remember what we call that? Yes! An erection!" (Here you can explain exactly how the penis works.) *"The penis is then ready to be put into the woman's vagina. Both the man and the woman can experience great pleasure when this is done. That is called an orgasm. The man's seed will come out of his penis and flow into the woman's vagina. We call that an ejaculation. If the woman is ovulating, which means that an egg had been released from her ovaries, this egg will be waiting for a sperm cell.*

"The last time we spoke about this, you couldn't believe that anyone wants to do that! You even pulled a face when Daddy and I kissed each other. But as you get older, you are going to experience sexual feelings in your private parts (we call them genitals), and then it will make more sense to you. I want you to know that if you don't understand anything about this or if you have any questions, even weird questions, you can come and talk to me—about anything! You might feel a bit shy talking about it, but guess what… I am sometimes a bit uncomfortable, too. But it is important that we chat about these things so that you have someone you can trust and talk to.

"So while we are on the subject of sexual intercourse, let me explain something called conception."

"Conception? That sounds weird!"

"It's not weird, it's the miracle of life! Conception is when an egg cell from the mommy and a sperm cell from the daddy joins together. This is when the miracle of life begins. This is when God starts weaving the inner parts of our bodies. That is the moment He puts His Spirit in us! As soon as the egg and the seed melts together, there is life! We say that the egg has been fertilized. A fertilized egg needs a place to attach itself so that it can get food and grow." (Use your line drawing to explain.) *"When this happens, it moves down to the side of the uterus and attaches itself in that blood lining that had built up. Now we say that the mommy is pregnant. If the mommy does not fall pregnant, this blood lining will come out through her vagina, together with the unfertilized egg. That's what we call menstruation, remember?*

"The baby gets food and air from the mommy, through the umbilical cord. The layer that had built up is providing the egg with a great place to attach to. It's super important that the mommy eats healthy, uses no drugs and alcohol, and doesn't smoke. Everything the mommy eats, drinks, and breathes goes to the baby. The baby will grow and grow and grow for about nine months, and then it will be ready to be born. When the time has come, the mommy will feel cramps in her uterus which we call contractions. At this stage she goes to the hospital where the doctor can help her, or she can choose to have the baby at home. When the mommy feels those cramps, it means the birth process has started. When that happened to me, it was one of the greatest days of my life. That was the day I met you!" (Here you can go into as much detail as you want, but maybe just keep the real-time video of you pushing your prince or princess into this world for a later stage... That is, unless you are raising your kids on a farm where they are used to seeing animals give birth!)

"If the time isn't right to have a baby or you don't want more children, you or your spouse can use contraception when you have sex. Contraception is medication or a device that helps you to not fall pregnant. There are many different kinds of contraception methods." (Here you can explain how a condom or birth control pills work. By giving them the facts about contraception, you are giving them the correct information, not permission to have sex before marriage.)

I suggest that it would be good to discuss other subjects such as oral sex with your children before they go to high school. It is something they are going to hear about at school—for a fact! Below is an example of what you can say.

"One of the things you will hear about is oral sex. That is when a couple use their mouths to stimulate each other's private parts. The fancy name for the stimulation of a man's penis is fellatio. It has lots of different names, even a few rude ones, but the most common slang names you will hear are 'blow job', 'sucking' or 'giving head'. The fancy name for oral sex performed on a woman is cunnilingus. Remember, oral sex is extremely sexual in nature and there is no guarantee that you will be protected from sexually transmitted infections. Oral sex is not a

replacement or substitute for sex, nor is it safer than sex. Any stimulation of the private parts, no matter how it happens, is sexual, and mostly leads to penetration. Rather try to avoid discussions about sexual stuff. You might get the wrong information. If you have any questions about this, please come talk to me."

There are many differing opinions with regards to the practice of oral sex. Many couples are for it and others are against it, for many different reasons. Let me just say that if your child ever has the guts to ask if it is something that you and your spouse are doing, then… uhm… you are on your own!

3. Teach them about the distortion of God's special gift

Yes, you will have to talk about the uglies as well: Rape, pornography, sexually transmitted diseases (STDs), orgies, abortion, adultery, etc. These are all things they are going to hear about at school and in the media. In the same way you discussed God's special gift to His creation, you can discuss how the enemy has distorted it. Here is an example of how you can discuss pornography, while keeping the 7 P's in mind:

"Okay, so we know that God gave us our sexuality as a very special gift. But you know what? God's enemy, the devil, hates this gift. He hates that it makes God's people happy and that it shows us how close God really wants to be to us. He hates that this special gift teaches us about God's passionate love for us, and he cannot stand it that this gift has the amazing ability to make marriages strong. The devil hates it so much that he decided that he is going to set us a trap. And sadly, because we sometimes listen to his lies and move away from God's umbrella, we fall into his trap. One of these traps is called pornography. That is when someone looks at another person having sex or doing sexual things in a book, on the computer or on a phone. Or even in real life. This is super dangerous and very addictive because it can give you sexual feelings that can be so strong that you have to act on it. Having sexual feelings is normal, but if we get it from looking at other people doing sexual things or showing their private parts, we can fall into the

devil's trap. That is how he tricks us. God says that sex is private and that it is only for you and your spouse. So we have to be on guard every day and protect our gift. If we see something like that by accident, like a naked lady advertising sexy underwear on a billboard, we must choose to rather look away. If we see even just a glimpse of people doing sexual things to each other, we must also choose to look away. We must remember that sexual stimulation and enjoying each other's nakedness are for our spouses only. We must always protect our special gift.

"Pornography also hurts everyone who is involved. It hurts marriages because it is like allowing someone else into your own bedroom. That is cheating! It disrespects the promises you made to God and to each other. It breaks the trust and the beautiful, unique love a couple shares. It also hurts the actors because they lose self-respect by undressing and performing sexual acts on camera for the whole world to see. Many of these actors have to dissociate their minds from their real selves. Some even have a no-kissing rule, reserving this special act for those they truly love. This suggests that they are trying to hold on to something pure while giving their bodies away.

"Pornography hurts children, too. Many bad people take pictures of naked children and force them to do sexual things on camera. These pictures and videos are then sold for money on the Internet, at the expense of these poor, helpless kids. That is sexual abuse, and those grown-ups will go to jail if they get caught.

"Pornography hurts women. So many women take part in pornography because they believe the lie that they are worth nothing or that that is the only way they will ever be loved. How heartbreaking is that? Some women believe that that is the only way they can make money and care for their families. Pornography makes these women feel worthless, as if they are just play toys for men. Sometimes these women are forced to do these things. Some of them have no choice because they were sold into it, and others are being raped, extorted, or blackmailed.

"Pornography hurts the viewers. The enemy uses it as bait and fuel for sexual addiction. It offers people an easy but sinful way to be unfaithful to their spouses

and loved ones. It makes the relationship with the opposite sex cheap and objectifies and devalues woman (and men). The more people that view porn, the more demand there is. That mean that the more people look at pornography, the more videos will be made with real people in it. So if someone watches pornography, they are actually contributing greatly to this business.

"Pornography is highly addictive and stronger than the strongest drug because it stimulates your natural sexual feelings. The porn industry is making billions of dollars every month.

"Do you now see how we, as humans, fall so easily into the devil's trap? He is using our natural sexual feelings against us! God has such a massive garden of goodies for married couples. Why spoil it by introducing it to a stranger who takes and never gives? We must be clever and ask God to help us fight this enemy when he wants to seduce us into watching porn or if someone pressures us to do sexual things. If you ever feel that you are struggling or if you just want to talk about it, please come to me so that we can fight this together!"

4. Teach them about relationships, romance, and dating

One Sunday, while I was preparing lunch, my husband went out for a run. Just as he left, the doorbell rang, but when I went to the door, no one was there. This happened a few times while I was busy cooking. A bit confused, I told my daughters to keep a lookout at the window to see if someone was trying to trick us, while I put the roast into the oven. It was not long before my daughters noticed not one, not two, but three young boys running away and hiding behind the hedge as soon as they pressed the doorbell. A sudden wave of motherly instinct caught me by surprise: Three boys showing up at our front door already! Not on my watch! I glared out of the window, trying hard to stare them down. It was game on and I was not planning to lose. Meat burning in the oven, whatever—my girls' reputation was on the line over here. Turns out that one of the boys is in my daughter's class and they regularly play together during break times. The other two boys are his brothers. I relaxed—just a bit—and told my daughters that they can go outside to play with them if they want to, and they ran out of the house utterly excited. Running and laughing they played hide-and-seek with the boys until they were all red in the face.

Later, when my husband returned from his run, I told him about my oh-so-shocking experience. He just laughed and said jokingly, "I just left for a run and when I came back our girls had run off with some boys? How long was I gone for?!" I laughed, but inside I thought to myself, "Wow, in the blink of an eye our kids will be all grown up. How quickly time has passed already. I was still wiping their bums just the other day and look at them now! It's almost time for all these puberty talks and then they'll be 18 and gone... And what if I didn't do a good job and what if a silly boy with a doorbell-finger wants to take them out instead of playing hide-and-seek in the garden?!" Then I remembered that I was right in the middle of writing a book about exactly those things, so I should have known better, behaved in an I've-got-this manner, and played it cool. But I am not so cool. I am just like you. I have the same fears and the same questions and the same reactions. Even though I had the training, attended the workshops, did the research, read the books, and prayed and prayed and prayed, I am still so scared that I will mess this up.

So that night I asked my Father about it. I prayed, "Lord, I know I should be all cool, trust in You and have all this faith that it will work out. I should be calm and collected and rest in You and BE STILL and all that stuff. I shouldn't fear and I shouldn't worry. But guess what? I am going crazy! These are my baby girls! I can't afford to make mistakes over here, God! Now it's just three boys, but when that testosterone kicks in, I'm telling you, Lord, you will have to hold me back because it's gonna get ugly." Oh, I let Him have it. I told God all the things I will allow and what I will not allow, all the rules I am going to make, and I told Him about all my worries, fears, and anxieties. I mean, I was also a teenager, a young woman, once upon a time. I know how a young girl's heart behaves. I told God, "Look at how I messed up when I was young!" I sat at His feet for a long time, voicing my parenting fears, past mistakes and my own hypocrisy, shame, and guilt. And finally, I shut up and opened my Bible. My heart was raw, and I was overreacting, emotional and scared for my girls. The fact that something as silly as three boys ringing a doorbell can cause this reaction in me was clearly something to be dealt with. (Maybe it was just that time of the month!) However, God led me to read John 6:1–14: The well-known story of Jesus feeding thousands of people with just five loaves and two fish. I thought by myself, "Really, Lord? This is old news and so not relevant in my situation. Just another one of Your miracles… Woohoo."

Even so, God—in His kind and gentle way—showed me something in that passage that I have never seen before. In the same way that Jesus multiplied those few food items, so He will multiply the impact of what we are teaching our girls. In the same way, He will take the little I have to give, those things that I think is not enough to make a change and make it so much more— more than I ever thought possible. In the same way, without fretting, worrying, or increasing my efforts and so-called wisdom, He will, in the end, multiply the work we have done and the talks we have had with our children. He will let the seeds grow and He will water the garden. I can relax. God does the multiplication. He grows the fruit. My job is to teach them about *Him*.

It was such a relief when I understood what He was saying to me. A massive weight fell off my shoulders. Even if my efforts are only worth five slices of toast and two sardines, that is what I have. Only God can make that take root, grow and multiply. Yes, they make their own choices, and they will mess up, but our children are really in His hands. Wow.

So what does this have to do with relationships, romance, and dating? The answer is: everything. If we parent our kids out of a relationship with our own Father and even if we mess up, God is always there to be their Father, and it is not solely up to us. When you have chats with your kids about relationships and romance, remember what God says in His Word about it. Let that be your guide to what to say and how to say it. We might have different sentiments about dating, disco parties, sexuality, screen time, marriage, mothers-in-law, how-far-is-too-far, fat-free products, parenting, politics, church, and coconut oil, but God's way is to honor Him in all we do and say… No matter what it is. He's 'got this'!

With that in mind, below is how I plan to have the boyfriend discussion, and I am going to keep it short.

"No boyfriends." (Easy!)

However, since we do not want to create a little rebel who will run off with the first guy who rings the doorbells as soon as she fills out her bra, we have to be a bit more subtle.

Let's try it in the following way:

"I see some of your friends have boyfriends. What do you think about it?" (Let them answer so that you can see where they are and how they feel about it.)

"Can I tell you about the first time I liked a boy? Oh, I remember it so well!" (Share your first experience of really liking someone in a special way with them.)

"I mostly remember how it made me feel. When he looked at me, I got all nervous and giggly. When he smiled at me, I thought I was going to explode on the inside. I had butterflies in my tummy for weeks! And when I found out that he liked me, too, it made me feel on top of the world! I felt so special and important, and I was the envy of all my friends. When he held my hand for the first time, my heart was beating so fast that I was scared that he would hear it! But after a few days he forgot all about me and moved on to the new girl in the class. My heart was shattered, and I cried for days! But guess what; a few weeks later, I started liking

another boy. And the same thing repeated itself, over and over again. I didn't learn my lesson.

"Some girls' and boys' hearts get hurt so badly that they struggle to trust anybody ever again. This cycle only stopped the day I met your dad.

"My point is, I could have prevented many of my own heartbreaks. One day, when you are a bit older, I will tell you about my biggest heartbreak and how it almost ruined my life. God doesn't want our hearts to break like that over and over again. It's not good for us and it can make us feel unloved, insecure and unworthy of love. And you know that that is a lie straight from God's enemy, the devil. If he can get us to believe that he knows we will always look for love in the wrong places. God loves us the most and will never ever let you go. He has the perfect person for you, but He wants you to first grow up and get to know yourself like He knows you. And even though you might find that you like someone in a special way, it is very wise to choose to just be good friends and spend time together with other friends. This is how you get to know yourself and others. These feelings you have will probably pass, so let's keep these feelings safe for when God sends you your spouse one day. Then you can give that person your whole heart and not just pieces of it.

"It's very wise to guard your heart until the time is right. It's almost like putting soldiers in front of the doors of your heart. Soldiers have two very important jobs: One is that they must keep the bad guys out, and the second one is that they need to protect the valuables inside. If you are going to hand out your valuables, I guess you need to start employing more and stronger soldiers! Remember, if you give a person too much too soon, they will fall in love with your hand and not your heart." (Dating and relationships will be discussed in more detail in *Part 3*.)

5. Teach them about peer pressure and how to resist temptation

This is a tough one, because you are just as likely to fall for it, even at your age. Everyone wants to fit in, even adults, and I can prove it: You rock up at a work function in a suit and a tie, but as soon as you walk in you realize that you are completely overdressed. Everyone else is wearing flip-flops, shorts, and T-shirts. What would your first instinct be? I bet you would take off your jacket and tie, maybe even roll up your sleeves (or pants) and make some lame excuse about just coming from another, more formal function... You don't want to stand out. You want to fit in. You don't want everyone's eyes on you. You want to blend in. You succumb to peer pressure—at your age—without your colleagues even trying to pressure you.

The same goes for your child. In fact, it is even worse at their age. Also keep in mind that boys and girls are different. Boys like to show off their skills, prove their manliness, are usually more competitive with their friends, play rough games, and try to beat and wrestle their buddies. They are designed to love adventure and to strive to be the strongest, fastest, and cleverest. From a certain age they will start showing off in front of girls and they will never, ever admit that they are also scared of spiders. They love to receive a trophy, medal, or title—it makes them feel like heroes. This is normal and healthy. Because of this inner drive, boys also tend to measure their abilities against one another from childhood straight through to manhood. So when your boy's buddies are trying something new that they believe will make them look more manly and grown-up, it might be very hard for your boy to stand his ground because he also wants to fit in, be accepted, and respected and prove his manliness. To have someone else judge him about his choices, outfit, music taste, hairstyle or brand of shoes can be the worst feeling ever! One day, when everyone else is looking at porn, drinking beer and swearing, it might be difficult for him to not join the cool crowd. I mean, the world tells us that that is what real men do, right?

Likewise, girls also experience peer pressure, but where boys want to be respected, girls want to be treasured. God made a woman's heart so different. From when they are young, girls want to wear tutus and tiaras. A girl fantasizes about her wedding dress as soon she exits the birth canal. Girls are always twirling and looking at themselves in the mirror. They want to be beautiful. They want to be pretty. Dress-up, dolls, make-up, and perfume; those are the things girls are interested in. They want to make themselves more desirable. A girl wants to feel loved, and she dreams about a real prince who will treat her like a princess, just like Cinderella. Even if a girl is more of a tomboy, her heart still has the same desires of being loved and being beautiful. One day, your girl will notice that those same boys she played with in the mud are now making her heart pump chocolates! It is healthy and normal. When your little girl's friends then try new things, like wearing super tight outfits with their boobs popping out, she might want to try it as well, because those are the girls who get attention from the boys. Those girls will hear the words, "You are so hot and sexy." The cleverer boys—those who have refined their smooth-talking skills, will say, "You are the most beautiful girl in the world, and I want to make you mine." Remember, their hearts are wired to respond positively to clever words such as that. Girls must be very careful of smooth-talking boys. It feeds the need to feel beautiful, desired, and loved. They want to fit in with the girls who get the attention, even if they get it by dressing provocatively or by drinking with the boys. The world tells us that that is what hot young women do, right?

I used to explain it in the following way to the teenagers I taught:

"Growing up is like a long-distance race that we are running. It is not a sprint. For sprinting you need to run really fast from the start. After 100 meters you are exhausted! Long-distance runners know that, if they want to last until the end, they need to pace themselves and not give in to the desire to run faster to keep up with the faster runners. If they run too fast, they will not have enough energy to finish the race.

"It is the same with growing up. You will feel the pressure from the other 'faster runners' to do things that will make you feel more accepted, loved, or grown-up. The faster runners will want to try certain things way too soon, like kissing, dating and sex. It is so important for you to then remember to run steadily and to pace yourself during this time of your life. Do not be tempted to try to keep up with

these fast girls or boys—the ones who have all the boyfriends or girlfriends, the ones who are at all the cool parties, the ones who try to look like the girls in the magazines. The girls in the magazines don't even look like the girls in the magazines! (My mom used to say, "Don't be pretty like them, be pretty like you!) *They are at risk of falling out of the race. When that happens—and it will—you will come cruising through, waving at them where they are panting for breath and licking their wounds next to the road. You will finish strong. How amazing it will be to know that you ran the race well, honored God in your choices, kept the rules, stuck to the technique of the game, and listened to the words and wisdom of your coaches (your parents and God) and that you have finished well! The fast runners (the cool kids) might never finish and will miss out on what God has for them. What a shame!*

"It is hard—the race and the temptations—but it is worth the effort and the sacrifices. Do you know what will make this race so much easier? The right friends: Friends who encourage you to walk in sexual purity, to stick to your pace, to help you up when you fall, to cheer you on, to pass you an energy drink along the way and to encourage you when you want to give in or give up. The right friends are friends who point you in the way that you should go and remind you of the way when you get lost. Positive peer pressure from the right kind of friends can make you finish the race with a big, happy smile on your face."

Teach your children that the type of friends they have will be one of the biggest influences on how they are going to run the teenage race. Teach them the difference between friends who are gold versus those who are simply gold-plated.

"Friends are like the game of dominoes. When you choose your friends, you are partnering with that specific 'row'. If one falls, they all fall. You might think that you are strong enough not to fall, but the only way to not fall is to stand aside and not be part of that row. How will you know if you have the right friends? Well, when they start saying or doing things that make you feel uncomfortable, guilty, or scared, then they are not good friends. A big red light will be if they start doing

things that you feel you need to hide from your parents. If you are a clever runner—one who wants to finish the race well—then listen to your coaches and ask your Father to help you to run strong and steady. He will give you what you need."

How do we, as parents, help them to resist temptation? This is something you need to talk to them about before temptation starts coming their way. How will they react if this or that happens? It is sometimes very hard to make the right decision when we are caught by surprise. Discuss beforehand the things they can say or do in specific situations, like when someone takes out a bottle of alcohol at a party or if there is a boy or a girl who cannot keep their hands to themselves. For example, if their friends start talking about uncomfortable things or they are passing a phone with inappropriate or sexual images around, they can excuse themselves to go to the bathroom. Teach your child to get some distance in that situation… and to take the other friend who is also uncomfortable along. If they are at a sleepover and things are getting out of hand, they can get up and go for a swim or pretend to answer the phone and then get up, go to the kitchen, and pour everyone something to drink. If it is really very uncomfortable, your child can send your previously agreed-upon secret emergency code message to mom's or dad's phone, which signals you to go fetch them right away. There is always a way out. But they have to choose it. Choose to move away from the other dominoes.

My dad always said, "You only have one name. Don't go looking for it the next day because it won't be where you lost it."

Benjamin Franklin once said, "It takes many good deeds to build a good reputation, and only one bad one to lose it."

King Solomon said in Proverbs 22:1, "A good name is rather to be chosen than riches …"

Let your children ponder these three quotes from three very wise men.

6. Teach them to respect the opposite sex

The differences between the sexes are massive. Our brains are wired differently. We perceive life through different filters. We react and think differently and need different things from one another. We should respect and accept the fact that we have different roles to play so that we can help and complement one another. Where I am weak, my husband is strong, and vice versa. I am good with administrative tasks, while he sucks at it—big time. He is good at handling emotional situations, while I usually can't stop crying. He is very decisive, while I struggle to make up my mind. I am a fantastic cook, and he is a fantastic eater. At night when we get ready for bed and I religiously work through my arsenal of cleansers, toners, face creams, eye creams, serums, and moisturizers, he just brushes his teeth. I need love above all, while he finds respect and admiration more important… I had to learn that the hard way!

The point is that men and women think and act differently, and have different needs, so teaching your children to respect the opposite sex involves more than just a few sentences. They need to know the differences between not only the physical bodies, but also the emotional, mental, and spiritual aspects. They need to know why God made men and women differently, and that both sexes have different needs and roles. In the end, we want to establish a deep respect and acceptance of who God made each one as a man or a woman, so that they can grow up treating the opposite sex with the respect and love they deserve. That doesn't only go for their spouses, but also for the people they will work with, their friends and their children who might be a different sex. Moms with boys, for example, need to realize that little boys already need to be respected and admired. Dads with girls need to understand that little girls already need to feel beautiful, loved, protected and cared for.

7. Teach them about the correct use of technology

Yes, technology is part of sexuality education, and it is obvious why. Together with our choice of friends, it is one of the biggest influences on our sexual behavior and choices today. Just think about smartphones, movies, series, sitcoms, music videos, the Internet, advertising, etc.: It is a visual tool of discovery and communication. If you do not manage it as the parent, it *will* become the parent in your household and it will manage you. Be strict about this one. Make your rules early on and stick to them. Do your research and be tech-savvy, or your children will outwit you. You need to up your game when it comes to the lingo, the gadgets, and the apps. It will be like having a second day job if you are anything like me! (I am technologically challenged.) Nonetheless, we do not have a choice. *You* are the parent, not "Hey Google", Siri, Alexa, the Xbox, the PlayStation, or anything else with an "i" in its name. (Did I even say all of that right?!)

As stated in *The Parenting Children Course* by Nicky and Sila Lee, psychologist Aric Sigman suggests that screen time should be limited according to your child's ages[16]:

- Under 3 years old: No screen exposure
- 3–7 years old: 30–60 minutes per day
- 7–12 years old: 60 minutes per day
- 12–15 years old: 90 minutes per day
- 16+ years old: 2 hours per day

"One major side effect of the technological revolution has been the replacement of age-old activities (running, climbing, pretending, making, sharing) with a solitary, sedentary screen-based lifestyle" (Sue Palmer, *Toxic Childhood*[27]).

Let's not lose sight of the importance of play.

LET'S GET PRACTICAL

STUFF TO DO:

- Teach them about the seen and the unseen changes in both sexes. These changes include not just the physical changes but also the inside changes: Psychological, emotional, etc. Boys and girls operate differently in these areas. We need to understand and respect the opposite sex so much more than we do these days.
- Teach them about sexual feelings, sexual intercourse, pregnancy, and birth. Tell them the truth and give them the facts, statistics, and Scriptures. Teach them about God's heart.
- Teach them how the enemy wants to distort God's special gift and how we can counteract it.
- Teach them about relationships, romance, and dating, because the world is also teaching them, and what the world teaches is not what God wants for us. (More of this will be covered in *Part 3*.)
- Teach them about peer pressure and how to resist temptation—and then also listen to your own advice!
- Teach them about the correct use of technology. Get up to date on the latest apps, gadgets, and lingo, and get to know how it works. Again, *you* are the parent. God put you in charge of that hormone-infused young human. Use your authority and use it wisely.
- If you struggle (and you will), remember who your God is. Go to your Father in Heaven, your Heavenly Parent, and ask for wisdom. Learn to hear His voice and to teach that to your children as well. It is the biggest gift you can give them.

STUFF TO TALK ABOUT:

- During puberty, I suggest that you answer any question, talk about *everything* and initiate discussions about sexuality and relationships often.
- When watching a movie together, pause when something comes up that can lead to a teachable moment, ask questions, and have a discussion. Once, when my youngest was eight years old, we were watching a sitcom on television together. The married couple started kissing and ran off to the bedroom. My daughter looked at me with big eyes, so I paused and asked her what she was thinking. With no hesitation she said, "They are going to put their privates together, aren't they? Then the mommy will be pregnant! Can't you and daddy go do that quickly so that we can have a little baby brother? I promise I won't let him fall!" (Clearly, my job is not done yet...)

RECOMMENDED RESOURCES:

- Let the Children Fly: www.letthechildrenfly.com
- A very insightful book to read: *Selfies, Sexts and Smartphones: A Teenager's Online Survival Guide*, by Emma Sadleir and Lizzie Harrison
- *What's the Big Deal?* By Stan and Brenna Jones
- *Love and Respect: The Love She Most Desires; The Respect He Desperately Needs*, by Dr. Emerson Eggerichs
- *The Parenting Book* and *The Marriage Book*, by Nicky and Sila Lee

SCRIPTURES:

John 6:1–14 Some time after this, Jesus crossed to the far shore of the Sea of Galilee (that is, the Sea of Tiberias), and a great crowd of people followed him because they saw the signs he had performed by healing the sick. Then

Jesus went up on a mountainside and sat down with his disciples. The Jewish Passover Festival was near. When Jesus looked up and saw a great crowd coming toward him, he said to Philip, "Where shall we buy bread for these people to eat?" He asked this only to test him, for he already had in mind what he was going to do. Philip answered him, "It would take more than half a year's wages to buy enough bread for each one to have a bite!" Another of his disciples, Andrew, Simon Peter's brother, spoke up, "Here is a boy with five small barley loaves and two small fish, but how far will they go among so many?" Jesus said, "Have the people sit down." There was plenty of grass in that place, and they sat down (about five thousand men were there). Jesus then took the loaves, gave thanks, and distributed to those who were seated as much as they wanted. He did the same with the fish. When they had all had enough to eat, he said to his disciples, "Gather the pieces that are left over. Let nothing be wasted." So they gathered them and filled twelve baskets with the pieces of the five barley loaves left over by those who had eaten. After the people saw the sign Jesus performed, they began to say, "Surely this is the Prophet who is to come into the world."

Perseverance is the hard work you do after you get tired of the hard work you already did.

— Newt Gingrich

PART 3

DON'T STOP NOW!

(AGES 12–18+)

Chapter 7

It Doesn't Stop Here—So Revisit That Goal

The problem

Many parents stop speaking about the birds and the bees when their children reach a certain age, if their child does not want to talk about it or right after a once-off talk about it. My youngest daughter, our strong-willed child, once told me that she doesn't want to discuss anything with regard to sex and that she will let me know if she has a question. Not even a week later, she started bombarding me with questions about sex every night at bedtime. It took me a while to catch on to her sneaky plan—she doesn't want to go to sleep, so instead she asks mommy questions about things she knows mommy likes to talk about. Clever girl!

The problem is, when parents stop asking their children questions and stop initiating discussions about sex, children will find the answers elsewhere. But why do parents find this topic so hard? Maybe they (and/or their kids) are uncomfortable. Maybe there is fear: What if they give the children 'permission' to have sex if they keep talking about it? What if they know it all anyway? Maybe they are scared to be asked about their own sexual experiences and, as I stated earlier, these are all valid feelings. Yet to be silent about sex will send them the wrong message as well, ESPECIALLY in their teenage years. This is exactly the time that you need to increase your discussions, build your relationship, and guide them through this very tough time of growing up. This is the time they are going to ask less and less questions, especially about sex. The effect of this might be that they will not receive the right information and they will be ill-equipped for the situations in which they need to make important decisions.

A few things to think about

- Let's say your lifespan is 80 years. Imagine a timeline with a zero at the beginning and 80 at the end. Most life-changing decisions are made between the ages of 10 and 30 years: choices about schools, subjects, study choices, drugs, alcohol, sex, relationships, jobs, and friends. The consequences of these choices can affect the rest of your timeline—how you are going to spend your life. Do you understand the importance of a good relationship with your teenagers, good guidance, and many discussions? You only have your children for 18 years, maybe even less! Your time with them is so limited, so your impact *must* be powerful during this short timeframe. Young people need all the help that is available to them in order to make wise choices, because their young brains are not fully developed until about the age of 25 years.

- Someone once said that the hardest part of being a parent is watching your child going through something really tough but not being able to fix it for them. That is so true! However, I want to add to that. What is just as hard—maybe even harder—is to actually be able to fix it for them but choosing not to, because it will be the only way for them to learn. Guiding them does not mean doing things for them or telling them what to do step-by-step every time. It means teaching them to do things for themselves, giving them sound advice, teaching them about consequences and letting them experience it for themselves. If you are going to bail them out every time, you might have to bail them out of jail one day as well.

- The teenage years can be compared to when birds are getting ready to leave the nest: They have been under your protection 24/7, but as they grow up, they must exercise those wings. That flapping will drive you crazy. Some will even try to flap themselves out of the nest (there is at least one of those in every household), but they are not ready yet. If they leave the nest too early, they are going to hurt themselves or be easy prey for predators because they can't fly yet. So, still some more flapping to do (sigh). This flapping can come in the form of mood swings, tantrums, and attitudes, but guess what?! They still need you, even though they do not think so. They need you now more than ever. Who else is going to show them the tricks of flying high or low, hunting for food, or hiding from predators? Now, while they are flapping to get stronger, is the time to insist on quality time, discussion time, and affection. (Yes, a hug and a kiss will still go a long way, even if they are as stiff as an ironing board while you try to sneak in that hug.)

So even though they think that their flapping is proof that they can fly, we know better. Even though you see them going through things that you cannot help them with, or you see them going through things because they did not listen to your sound advice and you cannot help them out—and, oh, that is when you will get the worst flaps—they still need you. Even though they are flapping just because they can flap (because they can't yet fly) or because they think they know it all, they still need your love and boundaries. It's the time of *starting* to let them go (slowly), but it's also the time to *not* let go of them. Your role has changed, but you still have the job to parent them. You are still employed.

That means that you still have to talk about sexuality, consequences, relationships, pornography, abuse, God, friends, etc. You still have to guide them, teach them, show them, be there for them, lead by example, discipline them... and at the same time start letting them go little by little. Those wings do need to get stronger so that they can leave the nest one day and raise their own flappy birds.

May I share a story of a very close friend of mine? Let's call him John. He was raised in a Christian home and school. When he was 17 years old, he was in love and his girlfriend fell pregnant. When it was time to tell their parents, they were both very scared because his girlfriend's father was an upstanding man in society, in church and in his town. As expected, her father did not take the news very well. John's parents offered their financial support, as well as their help to raise the baby. Her father, however, did not want any of it. Without telling anyone, he booked her a flight to London to have an abortion there, as abortion was still illegal in South Africa at that time. This schoolgirl had no say in the matter, and she was forbidden from seeing John. Three days later she was back home, as if nothing happened. They secretly tried to carry on with the relationship, but after a few weeks both of them knew that it was not going to work, and they broke up. Too much had happened and the big elephant in the room—the abortion—was never spoken about again. Some time passed and the 17-year-old schoolgirl grew up and went on to study medicine. She is a lesbian now and lives with her girlfriend, with no desire to have children. Not only did her father lose his daughter and kill his own grandchild, but he also lost any chance of ever becoming a grandfather and his bloodline has been stopped in its tracks. The girl lost her chance of having a family of her own. Her child, as well as a part of her heart, was forcefully removed from her. Her father died of a massive heart attack a few years later. So much loss...

What happened to John? Well, another girlfriend fell pregnant in his first year of university and they decided together that a secret abortion was the only way out. A few years after the abortion—after quite an explosive relationship—they broke up, graduated, and moved on to different relationships. When he was in his thirties, John married a Christian girl who had him wait for sex until their wedding day. When she fell pregnant a year later, John was super excited and ready to be a dad and meet his child. Yet he could not get himself to ever speak about his two other children who would have been nearly adults by then. For the entire first half of the pregnancy, he couldn't call his baby a baby, but referred to it as a fetus. I sometimes wonder what John thinks and feels every day of his life when he looks at his wife and his beautiful children. Did he ever ask God for forgiveness? Does the past bother him? Does it affect his marriage? Does his wife even know? Did he bury it deeply? What would their lives look like today if the babies were not aborted? Would they have graduated? What if they decided to wait for sex until they could get married and were in a better position to deal with the consequences of having sex? What if girlfriend number one's dad hadn't forced the abortion? What about the emotional and mental trauma that resulted in her choosing a lifestyle of homosexuality? Was it worth it? What if, what if, what if… We will never know.

After reading this and thinking about your own choices or those of others, do you think that this was God's plan for us? Do you think it was His plan for our relationships? The hurt and the pain that result from unwise sexual choices have the power to destroy us.

Sex is so powerful. It is powerful to a married couple and it is even powerful enough to destroy life.

I tell you this story because it is the same story of countless others who live with the consequences of their sexual choices. How could this story be different if John and his girlfriend were raised in homes where parenting sexuality was part of the parenting process? How could their story have ended if God's intent for sexuality was imprinted in their minds, if sex was treated as a precious gift and not a play toy ("that is just what young people do") and if God's Word was modelled and taught with love, respect, laughter and fun? What will our life stories look like if we make wise choices and try to honor God with our sexuality? What would your timeline look like? What do we want our children's timelines to look like?

The solution

We can't make our children's choices for them, but we can make sure that we, as their parents, are their biggest influence. We need to use our God-given authority wisely and make sure that we do not just leave it up to chance, up to others or up to our children to figure it out by themselves. I know that we will probably make mistakes. Look at Moses, the poor guy. God told him to speak to a rock, but rather he hit the rock. As a result, he was not allowed to enter into the Promised Land. We can argue that God was unfair, but you see, God does not have favorites. If His chosen leader messes up, that leader also faces consequences, just like the rest of us. In fact, the standard is higher for God's chosen leaders, because they lead other humans, and those humans belong to God. You, also, have been chosen to raise a spirit for God, a spirit that lives in a body with your DNA: your child. One day, your child's spirit will leave this earth and it can only go to one of two places. Where it will go depends on the choices made on earth. God gave you, the parent, about 18 years to guide those choices. God takes your job seriously. Do you? He is a loving and merciful boss, but He is strict, fair, and just. One day you will give Him account. What did you do with that little spirit He entrusted to your care?

Let me share this short anecdote: I am learning a third language. My tutor, a lovely 25-year-old lady, asked our class to speak about our Christmas traditions. As everyone in the class comes from different parts of the world, it made for very interesting conversation! We asked our tutor the same question. She replied that she has no Christmas traditions. Her parents never took her to church or taught her about God. There were so many others in our class, but my heart bled for her that night. I kept trying to imagine how different her life might have been if she had gotten to know Jesus, and what a special time Christmas would have been for her. I looked at her and felt a sudden rush of intense emotion and love, but also a strange sense of… sadness. I knew God wanted me to experience just a fraction of what He is feeling for her. I wanted to shout it out to her! And deep in my heart, a part of me blamed her parents. They didn't teach her about God. But God showed me that blaming her parents isn't going to fix anything. Me speaking to parents about God might, however, make an impact, because when parents get on board, most children will follow.

Our influence as parents should not be underestimated. Talks about sex, sexuality, private parts, and bodily functions should be as easy as brushing teeth and should be done just as regularly and properly so that there are no stinky breaths and rotten teeth later in life. It might not be the most comfortable thing to do, like flossing, but if you do not do it, the wrong information or lack thereof will cause plaque and tartar—hard to get rid of, might do permanent damage and you may lose a few pearly whites along the way. No one likes that piercing sound of the dentist's drill that feels as if it is sharpening your collarbones!

God's truth brings life. Let's talk about sex, people. Let's talk about our bodies in a respectful and graceful manner. Let's open up about our sin and bring it into the light. Let's follow God's lifegiving way. Know that parenting sexuality does not stop at puberty. The hard work is only starting! From the age of 10 years, you have about six to eight years left to influence, guide and parent your child's sexuality. Use this short, precious time wisely. A river cuts through rocks not because of its power, but because of its persistence, perseverance, and repetitive nature.

Let's revisit the goal

In the beginning of this book, we discussed in great detail why it is important to keep your eyes on the prize. At this stage of parenting, it is vital to remember these goals to check if you are still on the right track and if you need to make any adjustments. Just a reality check before we move on: Your goal might not be something your kids are going to get excited about, especially at this stage. It might not be their goal as well and they might ignore you and your oh-so-clever advice completely. Those days will feel extra-long and tedious, especially if you spend them on your knees, because the devil has a way of attacking us when we feel at our lowest. Yet those are the days that God will show you that He's 'got this'!

Goal 1

A lifestyle of purity: It is a lifelong process of teaching and modelling by you, the parent, and it starts when they are born. With a goal in mind, you have direction and intention. You will be more focused and deliberate in your mission. You know what you are aiming at. You won't get lost along the way. A goal keeps us on track.

Goal 2

Your job is to **prepare** your child so that goal one is possible. If your child receives no education, skills training, teaching, modelling, and repeating-repeating-repeating, the target will be missed!

Now that we are back on track, let us take a good look at other concepts that need to be in place during the teenage years. I have found knowledge of the following subjects severely lacking in most of the teenagers I was teaching:

- Why sex is a very big deal and why it is important to wait until marriage.
- The consequences of premarital sex.
- The need to practice self-control.
- Respect for and understanding of the opposite sex.
- Understanding what a real love relationship is—confusion about sex and love.
- The importance of having someone to explain sexuality on an ongoing basis; of having parents who talk about sex.
- The purpose of marriage and the purpose of being single.
- The connection between Goals 1 and 2 above, to getting the above-mentioned bullet points in place.

Do you understand now that your job is not yet done? Finally, your children are old enough to understand big words and they might even use those words in sentences! (Let me say it in a more acceptable way: They are finally grown-up enough to grasp the more complex concepts of their sexuality.) Now is the time to have detailed and wonderful discussions about sex! How exciting?! This is vital for their healthy development into adulthood where they will be people who honor God in their sexualities (which is goal number one). If that is the result, you will know that you have succeeded in goal number two.

Before you pop the champagne, however, there are still a few more years where you have to download some serious apps into their hard drives. Better get to work, then! Here are a couple of quotes to fire you up:

"Never, never, never, never give up." – Winston Churchill

"Will it be easy? Nope. Worth it? Absolutely." – Unknown

CHAPTER 8

TEACH THEM THE BIG DEAL ABOUT SEX—GOD'S INTENT

Just so that you also know, sex is not just for procreation and not just for fun and pleasure. God's idea when it comes to sex is something so much bigger than us. He has a purpose for everything! One does not put boundaries around things that are not important, which means sex is clearly very valuable to our Father. So why is sex a big deal to God? What is God's purpose for it if it is about more than just making babies?

1. Sex is for bonding

Genesis 2:23–24 The man [Adam] said, "This is now bone of my bones and flesh of my flesh; she shall be called 'woman' [ishah], for she was taken out of man [ish]." That is why a man [ish] leaves his father and mother and is united to his wife [ishah], and they become one flesh.

The following is a piece from Lois Tverberg, an author and teacher of the Jewish context of Christianity[18]:

The creation story has many profound things to say about God's intention for our lives. We can be enriched just by looking closely at the Hebrew words that are used to describe the first human Adam, and then the creation of man and woman.

It may surprise English readers that the word adam is a neutral term meaning "human", not specifically a man. In the original Hebrew text, all references to Adam are neutral until God takes some of Adam's flesh and makes a woman – ishah, in Hebrew. Only at that point is Adam called ish, a man. The Hebrew word ishah hints at her origins from within the eish, something that we can mimic in English, with the words, "man" and "woman." But interestingly, Adam is never called an ish until the ishah has been separated from him. It is as if the text is implying that male and female cannot define themselves fully as human without the other.

We may not realize that this logic is part of the next verse that says that for this reason, when a man and woman marry, they become "one." They are returning to God's first design before the ish and ishah were separated. The complementarity between man and woman is inherent in the way they were taken apart from each other, as the first ishah provided what the ish lacks. In God's design, it is the two together who ultimately reflect the image of God.

Marriage (sex) reflects God's covenant relationship with us. Marriage is not a consumer relationship; it is a covenant relationship. When a man and a woman come together in marriage, it symbolizes God's passion and His unfailing, faithful, unconditional covenant love. Our relationships with our spouses should reflect that love. (However, we do fail, and that is why we need Him so much.) Sex is the ultimate celebration of that intimacy. God wants to be *that* close. He lives *within* us. We become *one* when we engage in sexual intercourse. Sex is for bonding with our spouses, but it also reflects how God bonds with us, like Christ with the Church.

To visually illustrate the process of bonding with your children, take two differently colored papers and glue it together. That is how close God wants to be to you. That is how close you get to your spouse. God says we become one. Now try to tear those two papers apart. That symbolizes a break-up, a divorce, or unfaithfulness. The papers tear, leaving bits behind on each other. The pain of separation, especially after giving yourself so fully, can be very destructive. When a sexual relationship ends, there is pain experienced that God never intended for you to feel.

Sex was designed to bind marriage partners forever by releasing certain hormones in our bodies. Sex was designed so that you can be one with your spouse and to bond with that special person in a unique way, a way that is different from any other relationship. Also, just so that you know, these same hormones are released even when people are just kissing or hugging! It helps us to bond with our offspring. Kissing and hugging our babies is vital for healthy development, and so is kissing and hugging our spouses vital for keeping the relationship healthy. If we sleep with or fool around with someone who we are not married to, these hormones make us feel more connected to that person than we are supposed to be, as if we're one, when really we're still two. It even makes us stick around in bad relationships longer than we should. Bad relationship + sexual relationship = you can't win. Sexual relationships were designed to last forever. God knows what is best and His design is amazing. Let's choose to rather follow His ways!

If you choose to be single, you don't have that covenant relationship with another human being, so your relationship with *God* is then the focus and should reflect that covenant. If you are single, remember that your hormones were still designed to facilitate that bonding and you must be careful of who you grow close to. "Above all else, guard your heart, for everything you do flows from it," (Proverbs 4:23). You don't guard worthless things. You protect valuable things.

"But what if we love one another?" Or they might say, "But we are planning to get married anyway?" Or how about, "I am 45, divorced, and don't want to get married again!"

Well, it *can* be an expression of infatuation or even romance, but it is not love in the biblical sense of actively putting the other person's needs above your own. Sex binds us, not only to our partner's sexual needs, but to *all* their needs: Food, clothing, shelter, emotional well-being, spiritual well-being, all of it. When we view sex as an expression of *that* sort of love, then it's plain that anything less than sex within marriage cheapens the value of sex. If you're not willing to be so bound to someone that all his or her needs essentially become your own needs, then you shouldn't be having sex. If you are willing to accept that responsibility, then you should publicly profess that willingness before having sex so that other people can hold you accountable. That is why there are witnesses present at a wedding, of which the most important one is God (Malachi 2:14).

Remember, God's standard doesn't change just because you are a single adult, divorced, widowed, or over a certain age. He still wants you to wait for marriage to have sex. Personal circumstances and age aren't going to change His standards.

2. Sex is for having children

Genesis 1:28 God blessed them and said to them, "Be fruitful and increase in number; fill the earth and subdue it. Rule over the fish in the sea and the birds in the sky and over every living creature that moves on the ground."

God wanted godly offspring. He longs for more people to have relationship with. He sees children as a blessing (Psalm 127:5; Malachi 2:15). He wants to fill the earth that He made and enjoy His creation. The earth has been designed to perfectly sustain human life.

Unfortunately, Western culture has managed to largely separate sex from procreation. The original design of sex is ingenious—God made the most pleasurable human experience the means by which new life is generated. That puts an enormous responsibility on those engaging in sexual activity. Birth control has taken away the fear of unwanted pregnancies, but sadly it also makes it easy to treat sex like a game. If sex is separated from procreation, you separate the care for a child who might be a product of that sexual union (and also the care of the sexual partner). Thus, it is no surprise that child abuse and sexual abuse (in both children and adults) are proportionately more common outside of marriage than within. Without marriage there is no public agreement in place stipulating that each party of the sexual relationship must care for the other and any children who might be born out of it. Of course, abuse can occur within marriage, but not because the institution of marriage is faulty; rather because humans are slaves to sin (Ephesians 2:1–3). Is the idea of a car stupid just because my car is broken? Of course not! Yet if sex is acceptable outside of marriage, then sex and children are present outside of the context where a person voluntarily acknowledges their duty to care for his or her sexual partner and their children.

3. Sex is for pleasure

Proverbs 5:15 Drink water from your own cistern, running water from your own well.

Proverbs 5:18–19 May your fountain be blessed, and may you rejoice in the wife of your youth. A loving doe, a graceful deer—may her breasts satisfy you always, may you ever be intoxicated with her love.

Song of Songs 7:6–12 He: How beautiful you are and how pleasing, my love, with your delights! Your stature is like that of the palm, and your breasts like clusters of fruit. I said, "I will climb the palm tree; I will take hold of its fruit." May your breasts be like clusters of grapes on the vine, the fragrance of your breath like apples, and your mouth like the best wine. She: May the wine go straight to my beloved, flowing gently over lips and teeth. I belong to my beloved, and his desire is for me. Come, my beloved, let us go to the countryside, let us spend the night in the villages. Let us go early to the vineyards to see if the vines have budded, if their blossoms have opened, and if the pomegranates are in bloom—there I will give you my love.

In fact, just read the whole Song of Songs! It is a unique book in the Bible because it shows no interest in the laws of the Old Testament, nor does it teach or explore wisdom as in Proverbs or Ecclesiastes. Instead, it celebrates the sexual love between two lovers praising one another and yearning for one another. They are desiring one another and rejoicing in sexual intimacy. Now if God includes a whole book about it in His Word, then surely it's as easy as that. Enjoy your sexuality with 'the wife of our youth'. Celebrate one another and desire your spouse sexually. It is beautiful, normal, healthy, and supposed to bring us pleasure!

That is why you have to be positive and uplifting and make it fun and exciting when you have discussions about sex. Show respect for God's intent for sexuality and teach it to your children with a lot of love, affection, and grace. Do not shame sex or the human body. Don't be scared to talk, share or teach. Put it in its proper place and pray that your child will also one day, if he or she chooses to marry, have a fulfilling sex life.

Do not shy away from the 'private parts' as if it is a big no-no. Do you have any idea how many women struggle to accept their own vulvas? (Vulva is the collective name for all the external lady-bits, for example the vaginal opening, labia minora, labia majora, clitoris, pubic hair and a few other bits and pieces which are too hard to pronounce!) These women have reported having difficulty reaching orgasm, as well as difficulty in being intimate with their partners. They feel ashamed about their private parts and their own natural smells, sexuality, and desires. If you are one of those women, I want you to know that God made your body perfectly and wonderfully, and its desires and functions are normal and healthy.

Similarly, men can also have issues with their sexuality. Some men struggle with erectile dysfunction and other body issues such as size and performance. These issues are very real for some men and can cause great anxiety.

Please get help if you struggle to accept your body and the sexy bits attached to it. Don't project that shame and fear to your children. There shouldn't be any shame or fear. If there is, it's not from God and you need to sort it out. Take it to God (and your doctor, if necessary). Your husband deserves a woman who loves herself fully. Your wife deserves a man who loves himself fully. For the sake of your own sexual self, your spouse, and your children, it is your responsibility to get to a place of acceptance and love. Sexual pleasure in marriage is normal, healthy, and beautiful, and it pleases God. He also wants you to be pleased and to experience pleasure. People, you have no idea what you are missing out on! Go sort it out!

4. Sex helps us to avoid temptation

1 Corinthians 7:2–5 But since sexual immorality is occurring, each man should have sexual relations with his own wife, and each woman with her own husband. The husband should fulfill his marital duty to his wife, and likewise the wife to her husband. The wife does not have authority over her own body but yields it to her husband. In the same way, the husband does not have authority over his own body but yields it to his wife. Do not deprive each other except perhaps by mutual consent and for a time, so that you may devote yourselves to prayer. Then come together again so that Satan will not tempt you because of your lack of self-control.

Proverbs 5:15–17 Drink water from your own cistern, running water from your own well. Should your springs overflow in the streets, your streams of water in the public squares? Let them be yours alone, never to be shared with strangers.

Do you really think if you follow God and try your very best to obey Him, that the enemy is going to leave you alone? The answer is no. He will increase his attempts to steer you away from God because you choose another master. Sexual temptation is *everywhere* and we need to be aware of the fact that we are vulnerable, at risk and not immune to it. If you think you're not at risk, then chances are that you have some pride issues. Do all you can to ensure your own safety and the safety of your children. Teach them that even though they are in love and married, they still have to guard their hearts, eyes and ears. Sex within marriage also needs to be cultivated and protected so that the enemy doesn't get a foothold. You are responsible for your precious gift. Regular sex with your spouse assists you in being faithful and it lessens the chances of either party looking for pleasure elsewhere.

5. Sex is to experience the ultimate intimacy

Genesis 4:1a (NKJV) Now Adam **knew** Eve his wife, and she conceived and bore Cain …

Luke 1:34 (NKJV) Then Mary said to the angel, "How can this be, since I do not **know** a man?"

Matthew 1:25 (NKJV) and [Joseph] did not **know** her till she had brought forth her firstborn Son. And he called His name Jesus.

God created sex for intimacy (into-me-you-see). To know someone and to be fully known by someone signifies great intimacy. In Matthew 1:25 the word **know** is used as another word for having sexual relations with his wife. An interesting choice as it shows that having sex and knowing one another goes together. It shouldn't be separated. To reflect God's image on earth, you have to **know** Him. To be intimate with Him means you get to know Him more and more. Sexuality reflects that unique intimacy. It cannot be called intimacy without knowing one another.

6. Sex is a metaphor for the intimacy God wants with us

As discussed above, the gift of sexuality is meant to reflect God's passionate love for us. It is a visual representation and symbol of the blood of Jesus that flowed for us all—the ultimate passion move. That is why, when a woman is penetrated for the first time, her hymen tears, and a drop or two of blood might stain the sheet. It is symbolic of the curtain that tore in two when Jesus died, showing that man can enter freely into the holy of holies—into the presence of God—where new life begins. Blood was shed. The penalty for sin. Without it, there is no life. It is just like the womb, where life on earth begins. Your womb is only to be shared with the one you have a covenant with, the one who will, just like Jesus, give Himself up for you (Ephesians 5:25). How amazing and purposeful is our God!

LET'S GET PRACTICAL

STUFF TO DO:

- Parenting your child's sexuality doesn't stop when he or she reaches puberty. Now is the time to increase the frequency of your conversations and initiate discussions.

- Always include God's intent for sexuality into your discussions so that they understand that sex is not a toy, but a gift.

- Teach them that sex was designed for bonding, procreation, intimacy, pleasure (with one's spouse) and also to help them avoid temptation. It is good for a married couple and it is a precious gift to protect and enjoy within the safety of a covenant relationship: marriage.

- Always revisit goal number one: A lifestyle of purity—in *all* areas of life. Are you still on track?

- Remember goal two from *Chapter 2: Know Your Goal*: Prepare and equip your children with skills, values, character building and an intimate relationship with God. Think of this: What are you, as the parent, doing to instill these values? Are you deliberate in your parenting?

STUFF TO TALK ABOUT:

- Explain in detail every reason why God created sex. It is a big deal, and they need to understand why.

- Talk about what the consequences can be if sex is treated as something that just fulfills a physical need.

RECOMMENDED RESOURCES:

- Song of Songs in the Bible
- *The Act of Marriage: The Beauty of Sexual Love,* by Tim and Beverly LaHaye

SCRIPTURES:

Genesis 1:28 God blessed them and said to them, "Be fruitful and increase in number; fill the earth and subdue it. Rule over the fish in the sea and the birds in the sky and over every living creature that moves on the ground."

Genesis 2:23–24 The man said, "This is now bone of my bones and flesh of my flesh; she shall be called 'woman,' for she was taken out of man." That is why a man leaves his father and mother and is united to his wife, and they become one flesh.

Genesis 4:1 Adam made love to his wife Eve, and she became pregnant and gave birth to Cain. She said, "With the help of the Lord I have brought forth a man."

Psalm 127:5 Like arrows in the hands of a warrior are children born in one's youth. Blessed is the man whose quiver is full of them. They will not be put to shame when they contend with their opponents in court.

Proverbs 4:23 Above all else, guard your heart, for everything you do flows from it.

Proverbs 5:15–17 Drink water from your own cistern, running water from your own well. Should your springs overflow in the streets, your streams of water in the public squares? Let them be yours alone, never to be shared with strangers. A loving doe, a graceful deer—may her breasts satisfy you always, may you ever be intoxicated with her love.

Song of Songs 1:2 Let him kiss me with the kisses of his mouth—for your love is more delightful than wine.

Song of Songs 7:6–12 [He:] How beautiful you are and how pleasing, my love, with your delights! Your stature is like that of the palm, and your breasts like clusters of fruit. I said, "I will climb the palm tree; I will take hold of its fruit." May your breasts be like clusters of grapes on the vine, the fragrance of your breath like apples, and your mouth like the best wine. She: May the wine go straight to my beloved, flowing gently over lips and teeth. I belong to my beloved, and his desire is for me. Come, my beloved, let us go to the countryside, let us spend the night in the villages. Let us go early to the vineyards to see if the vines have budded, if their blossoms have opened, and if the pomegranates are in bloom—there I will give you my love.

Malachi 2:14–16 You ask, "Why?" It is because the Lord is the witness between you and the wife of your youth. You have been unfaithful to her, though she is your partner, the wife of your marriage covenant. Has not the one God made you? You belong to him in body and spirit. And what does the one God seek? Godly offspring. So be on your guard, and do not be unfaithful to the wife of your youth. "The man who hates and divorces his wife," says the Lord, the God of Israel, "does violence to the one he should protect," says the Lord Almighty. So be on your guard, and do not be unfaithful.

Matthew 1:25 But he did not consummate their marriage until she gave birth to a son. And he gave him the name Jesus.

Luke 1:34 "How will this be," Mary asked the angel, "since I am a virgin?"

1 Corinthians 7:3 The husband should fulfill his marital duty to his wife, and likewise the wife to her husband.

Ephesians 5:25 Husbands, love your wives, just as Christ loved the church and gave himself up for her.

Chapter 9

Teach Them About Consequences—Good and Bad

"You are free to choose, but you are not free from the consequences of your choices." – Ezra Taft Benson

If you were just a body, your only concern with regard to your sexual choices would have been pregnancy and sexually transmitted diseases and infections. There are numerous solutions on the market for those consequences, as well as legalized institutions that can take care of your issues, should you choose to go that route. However, you are not just a body. If you have any doubts about the emotional, spiritual, mental, and social aspects of human beings, just look at the people you know who treat sex as a form of casual recreation. What do their lives, relationships and emotional states look like? Are they truly exuding joy, contentment, and peace? When you have sex, it is not just your body involved but your whole being – your emotions and your memory, too. Mentally and spiritually, you are starting a process of becoming one with the other person.

Just teaching your children about the physical consequences of sexual choices will thus be an incomplete lesson, leaving out *most* of the consequences. We are going to take a look at the physical and also the emotional, mental, social and spiritual consequences of engaging in premarital sex—especially if the relationship doesn't work out or if it has been one-night stands or casual sex. These results reflect real experiences and feelings in teenagers and young adults from thousands of schools and tertiary institutions around the world.

1. Physical consequences

- Unwanted or unplanned pregnancies may occur.
- Risks include sexually transmitted diseases and infections, including HIV/AIDS.
- Early development of cervical cancer can occur, especially if multiple partners are involved.
- Sexual activity releases chemicals in the brain, creating an emotional bond.
- Breaking of the emotional bond causes depression in some cases and makes it harder to bond with someone else in the future.
- The chemicals that are released in the brain during sex can become addictive.
- The human brain is not fully developed until the mid-twenties and until then, it is harder to make wise relationship decisions.

2. Emotional consequences

The following unseen consequences are usually not mentioned by parents but can be very destructive to both sexes. That is why it is vital that your discussions include the following hidden consequences:

- Shame
- Guilt
- Loss of self-respect

- Loss of respect for sexual partner
- Anxiety
- Inability to trust
- Regret
- Fear
- Sadness
- Feelings of loss, being used, rejection, brokenness, insecurity, being emotionally unsafe, loneliness
- Many girls report feeling cheap, dirty, and used

According to Dr. Meg Meeker, a pediatrician and one of the USA's leading authorities in parenting teenagers and health, there is a direct link between depression and teen sex[17]. It was found that sexually active girls are more than three times more likely to be depressed and sexually active boys are more than twice as likely to be depressed. Dr. Meeker calls this a 'twin epidemic'.

3. Social consequences

- Low self-esteem
- Communication breakdowns
- Withdrawal from friends, family and activities
- Loss of trust
- Confusion between love and sex
- Confusion between acceptance and sex
- Isolation
- Sex possibly controlling the relationship
- Comparing self to others

Confusion between acceptance and sex occurs because when someone is sexually attracted to us, we may see it as proof that we are wanted, loved, and treasured (which is healthy in a marriage). The problem comes in when we see sexual attraction as the only form of real acceptance from another person.

Confusion occurs if a person starts to value themselves by the measure of sexual acceptance from another person. Many women wrongly believe they are ugly, rejected, and repulsive if a man does not want to have sex with them. So the opposite must also be true then… Many women wrongly believe they are only beautiful, attractive, and wanted if a man does want to have sex with them. So they give in. This confusion is especially prevalent in young people.

4. Mental consequences

- Low concentration levels
- Possible abandoning of school/university (dropping out)
- Affected studies
- Unfulfilled dreams

5. Spiritual consequences

- Feelings of shame and guilt
- Finding it hard to pray
- Withdrawal from God and Church community
- Hampered spiritual growth

A note on hampered spiritual growth: I heard about one college professor who said that when a young man comes to him struggling with his belief in God, the professor would ask, "Are you sleeping with your girlfriend?" He found that in almost all cases, the weakened faith was the result of sexual sin. Sustained sin causes our hearts to become hardened toward God and it dulls our spiritual impact – both God's impact on us and our impact on the world.

THE CONSEQUENCES OF MASTURBATION

The Bible does not specifically mention masturbation, but it does mention the lust of the flesh quite a few times! God says that our thoughts must be pure and that we must be careful of what we allow ourselves to think about. We must guard our hearts because the wellspring of life flows from it.

Keeping that in mind, we know that no one thinks of their mathematics examination while they masturbate. Instead, your head is full of sexual thoughts of all kinds.

A few consequences of masturbation are:

- It can become a habit which can turn into an addiction.
- Pornography and masturbation almost always go hand in hand (pun intended).
- It can cause you to feel guilty and shameful.
- It can lead to the real McCoy—sex—because masturbation will not satisfy for long. You will long for the real thing.

CONSEQUENCES OF PORNOGRAPHY

In *Chapter 5: How to Handle Those Uncomfortable Questions* and *Chapter 6: Prepare Them for Puberty*, I discussed pornography and how to discuss it with your children. This is a subject that you will have to refer to on a regular basis, because sadly it is part-and-parcel of today's society. Please read those chapters again and discuss it with your teenager.

A few additional consequences you can also include in your discussions with your teenager are:

- Pornography is more addictive than drugs and it can be very difficult to stop using pornography, because it abuses and takes captive the natural sexual feelings in your body. The human brain is programmed to produce certain feel-good hormones as a natural response to sex.

- It presents a false and distorted view of sex, sexuality, women, and men. The result is that you start to believe that what you see in pornography is what women and men want and need. You falsely believe that is the expectation from both sexes and you then copy what you see, thinking that is what sex and love look like.

- Marriages and relationships are ruined by pornography, seeing that it steals the trust between the couple, and it makes them vulnerable to look for the wild sexual experiences from other people.

- Your natural sexual stimulations are desensitized by pornography. Sex with your partner will not stimulate you enough anymore. It will cause you to seek more and more graphic pornography, because pornography will never truly satisfy.

- Pornography excludes love, respect, and intimacy from relationships.

- Pornography causes behavioral problems and early sexual activity during the teenage years, as well as an imbalance in healthy, normal sexual development.

- Getting aroused when watching orgies, threesomes or sex scenes of same-sex couples can make you believe that it's okay to have sex with a person of the same gender. This can lead to experimenting with the same sex and/or wondering about your own sexual identity.

- Children are abused through pornography because a demand for child pornography is created.

- Women are abused through pornography because a demand for sex trafficking is created. Pornography extorts women and children.

- Women also start believing the lie that they are worthless and that they are only sex toys for men.

- Pornography is a lucrative money-making business that abuses people of all ages, turning them into addicts and ruining their innocence, relationships, lives and self-worth.

- It makes you an adulterer and a cheater, seeing that you are bringing someone else into your bedroom. The actors and actresses on the screen know very well that they are being filmed, watched, and masturbated to by people across the world, both married and single. You're just not physically together in the same room.

- Online sexual abuse and harassment is becoming a normal part of everyday interaction. Sexual bullying has become a part of life for many girls who grow up in this digital generation.

- Pornography is molding and conditioning the sexual behaviors and attitudes of boys. Girls don't know how to deal with porn-saturated boys and are being pressured to do things inspired by the pornography that boys consume routinely and to put up with things that they do not enjoy. In a survey, one of the questions was, "How do you know if a guy likes you?" A girl in the eighth grade answered, "He still wants to talk to you after you give him oral sex." When a 15-year-old was asked about her first sexual experience, she said, "I think my body looked okay, he seemed to enjoy it."

- Girls in the seventh grade are increasingly seeking help on what to do about requests such as, "Send me a picture of your tits."

- Young girls are asking questions about bondage and S&M and they have started believing that being hit, being tied up and being stalked means that the boys love them. To these boys the word 'No' just means 'Persuade me.' [19]

- The director of a domestic violence center on the Gold Coast in Australia wrote about the increase in porn-related injuries to girls aged 14 and up resulting from sexual acts, including torture: "In the past few years we have had a huge increase in intimate partner rape of women from 14 to 80+. The biggest common denominator is consumption of porn by the offender. With offenders not able to differentiate between fantasy and reality, believing women are 'up for it' 24/7, ascribing to the myth that 'no means yes and yes means anal,' oblivious to injuries caused and never ever considering consent. We have seen a huge increase in deprivation of liberty, physical injuries, torture, drugging, filming, and sharing footage without consent."[20]

- Remember that all pornography websites—and there are millions— are run by adults, not children. If the adults of today are doing these things, our children are left vulnerable and exposed. Those who are supposed to protect children are the ones who are making children the victims. It is one of the most powerful weapons used by the enemy. Pornography is *not* okay, *not* normal, *not* healthy, and *not* 'just what boys (and girls) do'. Pornography steals, kills, and destroys.

It is quite scary and daunting to look at all the above-mentioned consequences, especially the consequences of pornography. You are 'just looking at it' right? How deceived we have become!

Parents, have you participated in any of the following?

- Emotional affair
- Pornography
- Adultery
- R-rated movies with explicit sex scenes or nudity
- Allowing children to watch sex scenes or other suggestive scenes in movies

- Fantasizing
- Sex outside marriage
- Unbroken soul ties from previous sexual sin

If you have, it is time to confess, repent, and ask God to restore you.

Confess: Tell Him what you did wrong

Repent: Turn from your sin and move in the opposite direction

Restore: Ask Him to restore what was lost, stolen, or broken due to sin

Lisa Max, from Let the Children Fly, wrote on her Facebook page[28], "For adults, we want to make sure we SHUT THE DOOR to sexual sin, but for children, we want to teach them how to NOT OPEN THE DOOR in the first place." That is why practically applying the principles in every chapter of this book is so important!

Why are all these consequences not being discussed with our teens? Are we as parents even aware of it all? Take a look at your own life: Have you experienced any of these consequences? I know I have! After the sexual relationship I had with a man who I was not married to, I experienced many of these consequences. It took me down a self-destructive path of eating disorders, and I had so much baggage that I was scared to fall in love again and my poor husband had to chew stones before I would eventually open my heart for him when we were dating. My parents sat by helplessly, watching me weighing less and less. Without God's patience and saving grace, I would have been in a very different place today.

Remember, your teenagers are full of hormones and they are experiencing new things daily. They are busy trying to figure out who they are and where they fit into this world. They are egocentric, want to be independent (like yesterday already) and anything or anyone can influence them at this stage. Long-term consequences are not yet a high priority in their minds.

That is why it's important to consistently teach and show them the consequences of one's choices and actions from when they are young. Teaching them that they are always responsible for how they act, no matter how they feel, is a life skill! Now is the time that it might just start to make sense. Even if it doesn't, you are planting seeds that will grow. When their values are clear to them, making decisions will be easier.

However, don't only focus on the negative aspects. Give them the advantages of waiting for marriage. This list is endless! For one, they will be free from all the above-mentioned consequences! Yes, there might be a few things your child can name that are not so cool if you do not have sex—such as getting rejected by your partner or friends, feeling lonely or being bullied because of your beliefs—but that's about it. I know that hurts. I experienced it all when I chose to wait for marriage, but it made me even more determined to fight the good fight and stand strong. I received such strength from God to resist the temptation that I can't even explain it. When ugly and hurtful words were flung my way, when people thought that there was something wrong with my vagina because I didn't indulge in having sex with my boyfriend, and even when some of my family members did not believe me, I just took it to God. I came back with renewed strength every time. Even some of my students found it amusing, abnormal, unbelievable, weird, worrisome... to name just a few adjectives. They would say, "But ma'am, you're, like, 30 years old!" (I only got married when I was 31 years old.)

Especially today, our children will be ridiculed and mocked by their peers if they choose to wait. Virginity is mocked and chastity is considered old-fashioned. C.S. Lewis said, "When the whole world is running towards a cliff, he who is running in the opposite direction appears to have lost his mind."

Let's raise our children to be resilient and give them the tools and understanding to run the opposite way and stand strong. Let's show them how free they can be, even in the face of looking crazy, abnormal or weird. This won't be easy, of course, but it will be worth it.

My dad used to say, "That which comes easy will not last long, and that which lasts long will not come easy." Going against the stream is going to be tough.

"A lie does not become truth, wrong does not become right and evil does not become good just because it is accepted by a majority." – Booker T. Washington

"Why fit in when you were born to stand out?" – Dr. Seuss

Let's raise a generation that stands out!

PRACTICE SOME COMEBACKS

I made a list of a few things that the world might throw at a child who is trying to be strong and to stand up. I also added a few comebacks to consider. Feel free to add your own!

The world says: Your sex drive is natural, so having sex is a biological need.
What you can say: *God has built in a mechanism for sexual release: orgasmic release during dreams. No record can be found of males being hospitalized because of girls refusing to provide sexual outlets. God also gave us self-control—a skill we need to practice from a young age. Children especially find this very hard…*

The world says: Everyone is doing it!
What you can say: *No, everyone is not doing it. There are thousands of young people who choose to wait. And I am one of them!*

The world says: If you love me, you will do it. Show me how much you love me.
What you can say: *Sex is not love. My sexual responsiveness is by no means an indication of my feelings for you. Love is not so selfish. If you love me, you will respect my boundaries and not cause me to go against my beliefs.*

The world says: I don't want to be inexperienced on my wedding night.

What you can say. *Getting to know one another sexually depends much more on communication than technique. It's so much more fulfilling to learn and grow together sexually in a marriage where I know you are committed, and I feel safe to express my insecurities and needs.*

The world says: We have to see if we are compatible sexually.

What you can say. *Sexual problems mostly arise when the non-physical parts of relationship are not in place, such as love, trust, good communication, friendship, and care. Intimacy comes through communication, not sex. By 'test driving' your partner, you mentally compare them to previous partners, which can make this partner feel insecure and threatened. It compromises the emotional safety of a relationship.*

The world says: We can still satisfy one another without having sex!

What you can say. *Mutual masturbation is definitely sexual in nature. Being sexual isn't just penetration! You won't be free of the consequences.*

The world says: We can use a condom.

What you can say. *A condom can't be put over your heart. A condom isn't 100% effective in preventing STIs and pregnancy, and it's not at all effective in any of the emotional, mental, social and spiritual consequences.*

The world says: We are in love and getting married soon anyway.

What you can say. *Loss of respect, guilt and dissatisfaction can be the result. It steals the excitement of the honeymoon. A break-up before the wedding can still occur. Research indicates that couples who live together without getting married increases the divorce rate of those who marry, and also reduces the number of those who do marry.*

The world says: Sex will bring us closer to one another.

What you can say. *Although feelings of intimacy are created by a 'chemical cocktail' that is produced in the brain during sex (which lasts for a short time), it is no guarantee that the deep emotional intimacy that everyone longs for will develop. In fact, premarital sex short-circuits the emotional bonding process, according to many studies. Most women linked their early sexual experiences to dissatisfaction in their present marriages, unhappiness with the level of sexual intimacy and the prevalence of low self-esteem.*

The world says: Scriptures about sex is outdated. It's not relevant for today's world.

What you can say: *Are the parts about stealing, murder, being kind and good and loving your neighbor then also outdated? Should we cut out the parts that we don't like, but keep the parts that suit our lifestyle? Scripture is eternal and God's standards of right and wrong don't change with the whims of culture.*

The world says: Let's watch this porn video together.

What you can say: *1) I am glad you asked! Hang on while I print out a copy of the consequences of pornography and let's discuss each one. Did you know we will be actively creating a demand for more sex trafficking? I don't want to be part of that!*

2) To quote Hamlet Act 3 Scene 3 Line 87 – "No."

The world says: You are conservative, narrow-minded, and religious. You are unprogressive, boring, a prude and a goody two shoes.

What you can say: *1) Thank you! And you know where the door is.*

2) I'm an acquired taste. If you don't like me, acquire some taste.

The world says: Why do you always say no?

What you can say: *"NO" is a complete sentence. It doesn't require a justification or an explanation from me.*

Can you think of more scenarios? Write down an answer and be prepared!

LET'S GET PRACTICAL

STUFF TO DO:

- Teach your children the consequences of premarital sex—not just the physical, but also the emotional, social, mental, and spiritual reasons. You can go into great detail and explain exactly the effect each consequence can have on their young lives and why it can be harmful for their development.

- Show them the advantages of not engaging in premarital sexual activity. Switch every negative consequence around, showing them the counter-blessing of choosing right. Show them that they will be *free* from all those negative consequences if they choose to wait!

- Teach your young ones to stand strong. Explain the following to them: It's okay to stand out, to be different and to stick to your beliefs. People might make fun of you, reject you or belittle you, but believe me, they are secretly admiring and respecting you. You are doing something they wish they had the strength to do! Your choice is in direct contrast to theirs, and anything that is pure and good will highlight the dark and evil opposing it. Your purity highlights their feelings of being dirty and having guilt and they don't like it. It makes them angry and jealous, so they belittle you. This is a form of peer pressure and manipulation. Teach them to recognize this form of manipulation and how to respond to it.

- Teach them that Jesus also stood out from the crowd. He openly disagreed with the religious teachers of the day.

- Make a list of questions, requests, arguments, and opinions that the world will throw at your child. Then think of an answer, decline, counterargument, and reason that you can use against it, write it down and memorize it. This can assist your children (and even other adults) to stand up and be prepared with an answer under pressure.

STUFF TO TALK ABOUT:

- Regularly discuss masturbation and how it can lead to the use of pornography. Teach your kids to always be vigilant and careful because porn is everywhere. It is highly addictive, and teenagers are mostly unaware of its dangers.
- Don't be afraid to tell them that we as parents must also be on our guard against pornography. Show them how to take their struggles to Jesus. Make them feel safe to come to you to chat about struggles in this area.
- Below are some more advantages of waiting until your wedding day that you can discuss with your teenagers.

EMOTIONAL REASONS:

- You will be protected from performance-based sex, guilt, addiction to sex and the hectic hardship of the break-up of a sexual relationship.
- You will instead be provided with maturity, intimacy, genuine love, respect and only one 'first time'.

RELATIONAL REASONS:

- You will be protected from unhealthy relationships, comparisons, sex-dominated relationships, mistrust, and the temptations of living together.

- You will instead be provided with a permanent, committed relationship which gives you a bond of love and trust.

SPIRITUAL REASONS:

- You will be protected from spiritual decline, sin against your own body, interrupted fellowship, and guilt.
- You will instead be provided with patience, self-control, trust, a closer relationship with Jesus and a clear conscience.

RECOMMENDED RESOURCES:

- *Hooked: New Science on How Casual Sex is Affecting Our Children,* by Freda McKissic Bush and Joe S. McIlhaney (this book is a *must!*)
- *Help! My Kids Are Viewing Pornography,* by Tim Challies
- *Struggle Against Porn: 29 Diagnostic Tests for Your Head and Heart,* by Benjamin Vrbicek
- *Porn Free* by John Bevere, on Messenger Courses: https://www.messengercourses.com/porn-free
- *The Whole Man Project,* available at thewholemanproject.com
- *The Conquer Series,* available at conquerseries.com

SCRIPTURES:

1 Corinthians 6:9–10,18–20 Or do you not know that wrongdoers will not inherit the kingdom of God? Do not be deceived: Neither the sexually immoral nor idolaters nor adulterers nor men who have sex with men nor thieves nor the greedy nor drunkards nor slanderers nor swindlers will inherit the kingdom of God. ... Flee from sexual immorality. All other sins a person commits are outside the body, but whoever sins sexually, sins against their own body. Do you not know that your bodies are temples of the Holy Spirit, who is in you, whom you have received from God? You are not your own; you were bought at a price. Therefore honor God with your bodies.

2 Corinthians 12:21 I am afraid that when I come again my God will humble me before you, and I will be grieved over many who have sinned earlier and have not repented of the impurity, sexual sin and debauchery in which they have indulged.

Galatians 5:19 The acts of the flesh are obvious: sexual immorality, impurity and debauchery ...

1 Thessalonians 4:3–4 It is God's will that you should be sanctified: that you should avoid sexual immorality; that each of you should learn to control your own body in a way that is holy and honorable ...

Hebrews 13:4 Marriage should be honored by all, and the marriage bed kept pure, for God will judge the adulterer and all the sexually immoral.

1 John 1:9 If we confess our sins, he is faithful and just and will forgive us our sins and purify us from all unrighteousness.

Chapter 10

Teach Them About Healthy Relationships— Set a High Standard

The world's way versus God's way

Visualize an upside-down triangle balancing on its tip. It's not very stable, is it? This is the 'Hollywood pattern' for relationships, as described by Dr. Darleen Edwards-Meyer, and it works as follows[21]:

1. Find the right person.
2. Fall in love.
3. Fix all your hopes and dreams on this person.
4. If it fails, repeat steps one through three.

We see it all the time: They look at each other across the room, they jump into bed and then they fall in love and get all infatuated with one another. They introduce one another to their friends and families, and then their relationship starts to experience the stresses of real life, which leads to them deciding whether marriage will benefit them or not. As you can see, the physical part of the relationship comes first with this pattern, but because the tip is at the bottom, its foundation is weak and can easily be toppled.

Following this pattern will cause you to set your hopes on finding the right person and then setting your hopes on the feelings to last. That person becomes the one responsible for keeping these feelings alive and if it doesn't work, you just try again… with someone else. In short, we call this dating. (Dating can cause a lot of heartbreak and emotional, mental, social, and spiritual consequences, even if the couple did not have sex.)

Dr. Edwards-Meyer suggests that we should use another model that is in line with God's will. It is a model that makes you a better person and eventually a better spouse, and it brings you into a closer relationship with the Lord:

1. BE the right person.
2. SERVE in love.
3. Fix your hopes and dreams on God.
4. If it fails, repeat steps one through three.

Does that not sound so much more… freeing? It's much more liberating, free from expectations and disappointments, free from performance and strife. I must say, if I knew this when I was younger, I would have made much different choices and saved myself so much heartache and pain. The above-mentioned steps put the focus on yourself and rather asking God to help your heart to change and grow, to help you serve and love the other person, and to make God your all. This should be done not just *before* marriage, but *during* marriage as well. This provides the best environment for a marriage to flourish. Imagine the result if both parties in a marriage do this!

So rather start your relationship with the triangle the right way up, with a firm foundation that cannot easily be moved: with your relationship with God as the basis and then moving towards getting to know one another. Then you see how each party operates and manages life and daily stresses and get to know one another's friends and families. Up until this stage, you will have guarded your heart. It is only when you reach this point that you should become emotionally involved and when that is in place, marriage and sex will be the most natural and easy outflow of the love that you share. This is what a healthy relationship looks like!

Dating

Why do we date? The scary part of dating is that you will either get married OR break up, in which case one or both of you will have a broken heart. If every date is a potential mate, then surely we should take this a bit more seriously. Jefferson Bethke said, "Dating with no intent to marry is like going to the grocery store with no money. You either leave unhappy or take something that isn't yours." Sometimes we just desperately want someone to love and adore us. We are sometimes so sucked in by the Hollywood model ourselves! We need/crave the approval and affection of the opposite sex to make us feel complete, and then we argue that it is normal and healthy and all part of growing up.

Is it?

Do you think God enjoys our pain when a relationship doesn't work out? Does He want us to get hurt and feel rejected and used just so that we can 'grow up' and 'learn'? Does He want to put us in a situation where our natural and healthy sexual urges will be tested to breaking point? Is that the only way to figure out what we need? I don't think so. That's not who God is! So why do we believe that having many relationships before we marry is the way to go if it only causes either ourselves or both parties involved pain and torture? Why do we think we can cut ourselves off emotionally but still have sex, or bond ourselves to many people emotionally and not be influenced? This will only result in us eventually becoming numb and desensitized. Why do we keep on messing with our hearts and the hearts of others and teach our children that it's normal and that they must do the same?

I think that God has a different way.

Dating isn't even mentioned in the Bible. Boaz didn't 'date' Ruth. Adam didn't 'date' Eve. Isaac didn't 'date' Rebecca. No, Isaac believed and trusted in God to bring him a wife. Her parents were respected and asked, as was Rebecca. He then gave her the nose ring (imagine that) and married her right there and then (Genesis 24). It was as easy as that; no ifs or buts. They got right into it! The sexual torture of waiting wasn't felt—they got married and had sex. Wonderful! (If only it was that easy today!)

One of the reasons why I think that dating isn't God's plan for us, is because we let our guard down and open our hearts way too soon. And as soon as we do that, we are much more likely to give in to sex. The modern peer pressure we experience as young adults to have a significant other can cause most of us to be depressed and sad if we are the only ones without someone special in our lives. We also climb the ladder of affection way too quickly, especially if we are dating someone exclusively. Because it's normal to be sexually attracted to one another, it's also natural to progress in our sexual advances toward one another. Sex is progressive in its nature. One of the most common questions I was asked as a teacher was, "How far is too far?" What would you answer your child if they ask you that question? What would you say to a friend who is single? Where is the line when it comes to your goal—living a lifestyle of purity?

Imagine a diving board at the Olympic Games. The swimmer climbs up the ladder to go to the top so that he can dive into the pool. With each step he climbs, he is getting further and further away from the ground. When he reaches the top, the next obvious and expected move will be to dive into the water. He makes the big jump. There is no turning back now!

The same goes for normal sexual progression in a dating relationship. It starts all innocently with the couple just holding hands, hugging, and embracing one another. It quickly moves to kissing and then tonsil-tennis is not far behind. Since French kissing has a way to really get the juices flowing, light petting—both over and under the clothes—will soon follow, and now that the private parts are being touched and stimulated, the most natural consequence will be sexual intercourse. So then you dive. You can't help it. Now you can't get back on that diving board. You have slept together. And you will do it again. Who would want to go back to just kissing after that? No one. You took that bite and it tasted good.

So how far is too far? At which step will your self-control not be able to handle the heat? I'm not saying that you should press your 'turn-up-the-heat' buttons to find out what the answer is! I'm saying that you should consider which of those buttons are sexual in nature. And if you are really honest, you will agree that it starts with kissing. So why are we testing it and constantly getting ourselves into these situations? Why is it that we enjoy torturing ourselves and, in the end, giving up and giving in?

Dating someone exclusively makes all of the above a very big possibility, almost a certainty. You will find yourself alone with that person more and more, and one thing will naturally lead to the next.

Before you make your choice with regard to how far is too far, let's have a look at what the clever people say about hormones.

Let's get chemical—Cupid's cocktail

Remember the last time you bumped into someone you found attractive? Sweaty palms? Some stammering? Heart pounding? You might even have said something so dumb that it didn't make sense at all. (Or is that just me?) No wonder that for centuries people thought love came from the heart.

There is a reason that the movies call it 'falling in love', because we hardly have any control over those amazing feelings that overtake our sanity. But just so you know, those wonderful and powerful feelings we want to give all the credit, are actually chemicals produced by our own bodies that flood the brain... not the heart.

We can divide romantic love into three categories, namely sexual desire, attraction, and attachment:

Sexual desire

The main culprits here are testosterone and estrogen. Our libido is driven by our desire for sexual gratification—which is a good thing. I mean, without these hormones helping us along, we wouldn't want to reproduce at all. Our hypothalamus (yeah, I know, what a word) is located in our brains and it stimulates the production of these earthshaking chemicals from our testes and ovaries, starting around puberty. These specific hormones influence our libido, thus driving our sexual desire, which—along with attraction—shut off the prefrontal cortex of the brain. This part of the brain controls rational behavior. That might explain the behavior of a certain Shakespearian couple we all know about!

Attraction

The hormones that rule this category are dopamine (famous for his headlining role in addiction), norepinephrine (the one that makes us less likely to eat and sleep) and serotonin (our mood-enhancers). The clever name for this threesome is 'monoamines' – *monos* for short.

Attraction is the love-struck phase and is quite tricky. We can lust for someone we are attracted to and vice versa. But one can also happen without the other! Attraction involves the brain pathways that control 'reward' behavior, which partly explains why the first bit of a new relationship can be so all-consuming.

Dopamine is a very interesting fellow. Also produced by the hypothalamus, he makes sure we feel gooooood—definitely one of the best players in the brain's reward pathway. He primes the brain to react to rewards in the making, such as food, drugs, hugs, and sex. So when we do things that we like, such as eating cake, gaming, spending time with loved ones or having sex, dopamine makes sure we enjoy the experience. It is also activated by the use of certain drugs, such as cocaine and nicotine. He also plays a role in movement, motivation, mental focus and even the production of breastmilk! Everyone wants to be dopamine's friend.

Next on the list is norepinephrine, also known as adrenalin. (This one plays a big role in the 'fight or flight' response, which kicks into high gear when we're stressed or in danger.) He makes us giddy, energetic, euphoric, while decreasing our appetite and giving us insomnia and sweaty palms... Sound familiar? (And you thought it was your sweetheart's fault!)

The last of the *monos* is serotonin. Serotonin has a wide variety of functions in the human body. People sometimes call it the happy hormone because it contributes to well-being and happiness. It appears to play a role in mood, emotions, appetite, and digestion. As the precursor for melatonin, it helps regulate sleep-wake cycles and the body clock.

The most shocking part is that when you are high on love, these chemicals deactivate the amygdala, which controls the perception of fear, anger, and sadness. No wonder you feel so safe and secure with the object of your affection. Your love can do no wrong in your eyes! At the same time, the brain dampens the ability of the mid and frontal cortex to use logic, criticize or think clearly, making you unable to analyze and judge your other half.

It doesn't take a matchmaker to see where this is going[22]. You are officially high on love, just like a drug addict, and you are going to want more. Addicted much? If you are not in love after such a hormonal hurricane, you will be soon.

Attachment

While sexual desire and attraction are pretty much exclusive to romantic entanglements, attachment is what you need for real friendship, parent–

infant bonding, and marriage. The two hormones responsible for making us commit to one other are oxytocin and vasopressin.

The brain seals the deal with oxytocin, the 'cuddle-hormone'. And boy, does it stay true to its nickname. It is produced by the hypothalamus in big quantities during hugging, kissing, sex, orgasm, breastfeeding, and childbirth! It helps cement the strong bond between mother and child, as well as helping a father bond with his offspring. It promotes bonding when adults are intimate and strengthens social bonds in mammals. Oxytocin influences relaxation and trust, and it decreases stress and anxiety when released into certain parts of the brain. This jack of all trades is also linked to fidelity: It causes males to see their partners as more attractive than other females, thus reducing infidelity.

Vasopressin is associated with physical and emotional mobilization and helps support vigilance and behaviors needed for guarding a partner or territory, as well as other forms of adaptive self-defense.

So...

Now that we understand cupid's chemical cocktail, we also need to look at what happens to these hormones when, well, it suddenly stops being produced in these big quantities, such as during a break-up. Dare we say that, just like an addict, we will suffer withdrawal? The pain we experience with a break-up is also to blame on the 'lack' of these hormones and can have severe consequences. Remember, all these chemicals are naturally present in our bodies and are there for our survival. They get produced even if we're not having sex. So even if you are just hugging, the hormones are being released. It is value-free, which means that even if you do dangerous things, or things that are not good for you, they will still be released. That means that it's possible to get attracted and attached to people or things that are not good for us.

Another thing to consider is that the world's attitude towards sex has changed. Much of what was seen as taboo thirty years ago is not taboo anymore. Teens know that adults have sex outside marriage, and they understand the sexual references made in much of the advertising that surrounds them. Most of the time these are connected to lust, rather than the traditional values of love.

Now, combine all of the above information about our natural release of hormones with the fact that today's views about sex and sexuality in the world has changed so much, and what do you get?

That's right: A PROBLEM. It's no surprise that teens are following the trends, taking part in sex earlier, experimenting with things they never would have, and then thinking we are the antique-convent-conservatives! It leaves us as parents with two big dilemmas: 1) How do we as Christian parents do this job of parenting a hormone-infused teenager in the area of sexuality? 2) How can we still be cool in the face of a teenager?

Lucky for you, I have the answer.

But only for the first dilemma...

To be cool in the eyes of a teen is impossible.

Interesting, is it not? God wired us in such a way that His purpose for sexuality can happen naturally. If we are aware that we can easily be led by our natural desires, we can be more careful when it comes to making our choices about dating and relationships.

The solution? Well, it depends on your goal, doesn't it? To maintain a lifestyle of purity, you must draw the line very clearly from the beginning, from the first step. Ask yourself the following questions:

1. Am I going to date or not? Or am I just going to stay friends, make more friends, and go out in groups so that I can get to know myself and others? (No matter your age.)

2. If I do choose to date exclusively and thus end up being alone with that person most of the time, what protective measures will I put in place to ensure that we don't start climbing that diving board? (Again, no matter your age!)

If you are serious about protecting your heart, I suggest you think it through and decide on your answers to these questions beforehand. You don't make the decision to turn down the heat while you are busy turning it up.

My love story

My husband and I had been friends for seven years before we showed any interest in one another. (Well, he always had some interest in me, to be honest.) But for most of those years, I struggled with bulimia and wasn't in the right state of mind for a relationship. It was only when my bulimia came to an end that I felt ready to accept any attention from a man, or so I thought. My dad was of the opinion that I was difficult and that I didn't know what I wanted. "Dad, please just let it go; not everyone knows how to drive a Ferrari," I would respond often. Since my dad was a big sports fan, we kind of had our own secret language when it came to boys.

Meanwhile, my parents knew nothing of my struggle with bulimia. In fact, I lied about it, big time. That is what you do when you feel too ashamed to tell people that you put your finger in your throat a few times every day. Those were hard times, and I wasted a big part of my twenties—what should have been the young and wonderful twenties. Thank the Lord that the eating disorder stopped (long story for another book…) and I could finally move on with my life.

Around that time, Ray, former game ranger and chiropractic student (and now my husband), started pursuing me. One morning, as I was eating breakfast (like a good old eating disorder-free girl does), the following message appeared on my phone: "Option 1: You come to the bush and we start a fantastic new life together. Option 2: I come to Cape Town and win your heart over. Option 3: No other option."

Well, well, well…

I ran to my housemate's room, eyes bigger than the eggs on my plate, to show her this sudden change of events. I mean, I had known that he liked me, but I didn't know that he LIKE-liked me! We giggled until early the next morning… and that at the age of 30! (Just to clarify, Ray and I lived a two-hour flight away from one another.) My conclusion was that I clearly had no choice, and soon we started visiting one another every few weeks, flying up and down, checking one another out.

I wish I can say that "the rest was history", but I can't. The start of our long-distance relationship was tough, not so much because of the distance, but because of my past relationship with Ed (short for eating disorder). Ed and I were together for five years. Ed hurt me. And Ed didn't want to let go. I was too afraid to open my heart again. My unaffectionate behavior was hard on Ray, and our relationship almost didn't make it.

One day, during one of our visits, we were at the Kruger National Park for a day trip. Ray was still a game ranger in his free time and knew a lot about the environment and the animals, so I loved to listen to his stories and to him sharing his knowledge. It was a late afternoon drive, and I was very sleepy. I lay with my head on his lap during the long drive back home. It was hot and the sun was shining on my face. As I drifted in and out of sleep, I noticed his hand trying to shield my eyes from the sun—for the whole duration of the drive back home. I pretended not to notice and to still be asleep. But never in my life had I felt that beautiful or that protected, even if it was just from the sun.

I got on the plane with a completely different outlook of this man. I had to invite him to visit me a few weeks later, of course. It was time to really get to know one another. I picked him up at the airport in Cape Town and we did some sightseeing, visiting wine farms and local restaurants. We chatted away, me wondering all the while why he suddenly looked so stupidly handsome?! He must have been working out, or maybe the wine was getting to me… Those broad shoulders looked extra-broad that day.

That same afternoon, he asked me to be his girlfriend in my town's local fish market. (While I was chewing on a piece of calamari!) His intentions were clear: He had future-wife ideas. After I had another sneaky look at those broad shoulders, I said yes. Yet that same old niggling feeling of fear immediately started haunting me, always in the backroom of my heart. Even though Ed wasn't physically part of me anymore, it was still trying to overwhelm me psychologically, and it was making me scared to fall in love again.

It took me a few months to finally deal with my issues, and after some time I was able to open my heart again. I needed that time to 'put down' my baggage. When I finally came around, I realized what a special man I had waiting for me: A man who actually loves me enough to help me unpack my baggage. He had been willing to patiently wait every time that I didn't return his love and affection. He backed off when I needed space, and he was right there when I needed him. I had found a man who, even though I gave him nothing in return during the first few months of our relationship, kept praying silently that I would notice his broad shoulders again.

His prayers were answered. It hit me one day while we were on a camping trip. I was looking up at him, and the sun was shining in my eyes. He moved so that his shadow could shield my face. I realized there that this man would always try to keep the sun out of my eyes, no matter what. He will always try to protect me. And my heart blossomed. I opened the back door in my heart, and the fear left. And the front door swung wide open.

It was game on!

Because we lived in different cities and we had to stay over with one another during our visits, we had to put a few ground rules in place. As our relationship progressed, we talked about sex a lot and made the decision to wait for our wedding day because of our beliefs. Some people might think that it was easier to control ourselves because the relationship was a long-distance one, and for some parts that might be true, but we had all the same temptations other couples have when we were together. We decided that he would sleep on the couch—right next to the washing machine! (Poor man; what he wouldn't do for love!) We discussed our 'rule' quite often, and it was clear that our desire for one another was very healthy and normal, and maybe even a little dangerous because of the fact that we both had sexual relationships with other people before. We had to make a rule, otherwise we could have faltered. But boy, are we glad that we waited for our wedding night. All I'm going to say is that it was definitely worth the wait!

You see, our love story is not perfect, and our relationship almost did not make it in the beginning. Sex would have complicated everything even more, especially with me being so fully packed with past baggage. Most people have baggage from the past, and we take it all into our consequent relationships. Add sex to that equation, and it can become quite the mess! Sex has the tendency to blind us from seeing the baggage that needs to be dealt with.

Young adults, especially, are in search of the greatest love story: being whisked off into a fairy tale, Hollywood-style idealistic romance, with passionate sex being had all the time. Yet God wants to teach us something very special: He says we must WAIT some time, instead of WASTE our time. In Song of Solomon, we are warned not to awaken love until it so pleases (Song of Songs 2:7). There are many ways in which we awaken love too soon. Some of those ways include social media, books, music, movies, and friends, to name a few. We are exposed to it every day and it awakens desires in us to the point that we do not want to wait patiently anymore.

Discuss these concepts with your children and let them think about the answers. Let them also come up with ideas about how to set boundaries, for example deciding in advance that dating might not be conducive to the wellness of their hearts. Your child can go out with friends in a group and get to know their peers during daily activities, even if there is a special person in the group who makes their heart beat faster. The best way to get to know that special person is to get to know him or her with others also around. It is very hard to wear a mask and pretend in front of your own friends and family, because they will call you out on it and the real you will be revealed.

We live in a time where sex, dating, one-night stands, making out, sex before coffee, oral sex before kissing, living together and sleeping over has become the norm. Our kids are exposed to much more than you think. You have to be deliberate in your conversations and make sure that they understand what is at stake.

I know that not dating or to only date when it is the person you intend to pursue for marriage is not the popular viewpoint. It is also a hard one to teach your teenagers. However, as C.S. Lewis said, "I didn't go to religion to make me happy. I always knew a bottle of Port would do that. If you want a religion to make you feel really comfortable, I certainly do not recommend Christianity." Our comfort is not at the top of God's priority list, but our hearts are. His Word is for our protection. His hand is there to keep the sun out of our eyes. If we choose to follow His map for our lives, it's only wise to listen to His directions, even if it is hard or unpopular (John 16:33).

Living together

The fancy word is 'co-habitation'. It means to live together as if you are married, just without the signed piece of paper that protects your rights, without the promises made to one another and to God, and without the witnesses, wedding party and white dress.

For some people, this is a convenient way to get what they want without commitment. For others, it is a solution to financial issues. For those with trust issues, living together is a permanent testing ground to see if the other person can live up to their standards and idyllic view of relationships: "We have to see if we are compatible! Who buys a car without driving it first?" In the end, both of them can satisfy their sexual desires while still checking to see if the other person is worthy of the time, money, and effort. Or maybe they do truly love one another, but they feel the concept of marriage is outdated, or that a signed piece of paper just complicates things.

I understand some of those reasons but know this one thing... Living together is a counterfeit to the real thing, namely marriage. It's like having a copy of a Leonardo da Vinci painting: you don't own the real painting. You have a fake in your house, and you pretend that it is the real deal, and everyone knows it. Actually, you don't even have to pretend, because so many others own fakes as well. It's just accepted as normal. The real thing costs too much. If anything happens to your fake, it does not matter, because it was cheap and can easily be replaced. There is no real value, and it is easy to let go of, just like someone you are not truly committed to.

When a sexual relationship becomes the focus, other important, non-sexual aspects diminish. Poor character traits, personality flaws and other problems are overlooked, but they will surface later on.

Research about the effect of co-habitation on marriage shows:

- Increased risk of breaking up after marriage
- Greater marital conflict
- Lower levels of happiness and well-being than in married couples
- Poorer communication
- Lower levels of sexual connection and satisfaction
- Poorer relationships with parents
- Increased rates of depression within marriage

It has also been found that living together results in the same physical, emotional, spiritual, social, and mental consequences as the consequences discussed in *Chapter 9: Teach Them About Consequences*. As found by research, abuse, rejection, and depression is four times more likely in marriage if the couple lived together before marriage.

The benefits of a healthy marriage have been researched extensively and it has been proven that marriage is the better way—God's way:

- Marriage enhances greater well-being.
- Married people:
    - are physically and mentally healthier.
    - live longer on average.
    - have more fulfilled lives.
    - take better care of themselves.
- Marriage provides more stability for children of the couple.

Just a short note: The benefits of marriage do not explain the high divorce rate. Hard hearts do. Hardened hearts in marriage are the biggest reason for divorce. From a hard heart flow many selfish behaviors.

When children reach the age of going to college or university, dating, and living together will cross their paths. It is important to discuss this topic often and openly, so that they can start thinking about their own choices in this regard. They will be pressured from many sides, so they need to decide where they stand, what their boundaries are and why. When kids are between the ages of 18 and 23, that is when parents have the most praying to do, in my opinion! They have reached adulthood and those wings are going to take them places. Gone are the bum wipes and the tantrums, the eye rolling and the door slams. They are now going to make their own choices and mistakes. We as parents have the opportunity to have such an impact on the sexual choices they will make one day. Let us not become tired of doing what is good. At exactly the right time we will reap a harvest of blessing if we do not give up (Galatians 6:9). Remember, the day you plant the seed is not the day you eat the fruit. Keep on investing in your children by talking about these concepts often.

Why is waiting important?

Iain Duguid, a professor at the Westminster Seminary in Philadelphia, wrote an article which I think expresses beautifully why waiting is so important:

Waiting to Awaken Love, by Iain Duguid[23]

One of the agonizing aspects of being in love but not yet married is the need to wait. You long for the day when your lives will be so intertwined that every aspect will be linked together, including sexually. This agony is not helped by the fact that we live in a sex-saturated culture where our eyes and minds are bombarded on all sides by the message that your sexuality is simply another appetite to be satisfied, like hunger and thirst. In such a context, it is easy to imagine that you are the only one waiting for sex until you are married.

Into this cauldron of unfulfilled desire the Song of Songs speaks with calm and reassuring wisdom when it says to the young women of Jerusalem, "Do not stir up or awaken love until it pleases." This caution is so important to the Song's portrayal of the beauty and power of love that it is repeated three times (Song of Solomon 2:7; 3:5; 8:4). This repetition is not because the Song has reservations about the goodness of love and sex in its proper place, within marriage. On the contrary, it depicts and praises the breathtaking intensity of a unique, lifelong, committed relationship between one man and one woman — what we might call, "friendship on fire."

Reasons, Not Just Rules

The way in which the Song persuades us to wait for marriage to have sex is striking, however. Often Christians focus on the various rules that the Bible gives us about our sexuality — the "Thou shalt not's." There is certainly biblical wisdom behind those rules. Yet what the Song adds to the rules are reasons. Rules are like walls and fences: They can mark out where proper boundaries exist. Yet walls and fences are of only limited help in keeping people in their proper place: they can easily be tunneled under, climbed over, or broken down. It is much more likely that we will stay on the proper side of the wall until marriage if we have a reason rather than simply a rule.

Intriguingly, the Song compares waiting for marriage to guarding a vineyard. In the springtime of the year, when flowers are in bloom and all nature is telling you to go forth, be fruitful, and multiply, the woman warns us of the little foxes that can damage the fragile blossoms of the vineyard, with serious long-term consequences for its fruitfulness (Song of Solomon 2:15). She reminds us that the farmer who invests his energy in protecting the integrity of the vineyard will not regret it later, even though the benefits of this painful perseverance won't be reaped until the time is fully ripe.

Tend the Vineyard

Vineyard tending is a long, patient process of waiting and watching in which one failure doesn't bring the whole endeavor to nothing. The farmer who fails doesn't have to give up the vineyard as damaged goods. He can repent and rebuild the broken wall and start again to watch and wait. Equally, while keeping the walls is important in vineyard tending, it is not the only thing. It's about taking care of tender blossoms. Tending your sexual vineyard is therefore not simply about actual physical sexual intercourse; it is about protecting your mind from habitual lust, romantic fantasy, and pornography, all of which can have long-term damaging effects. You can have a vineyard whose walls are still intact but whose blossoms have been trampled into the muddy dirt in other ways.

Nor is watching over the vineyard an end in itself. Rather, its wonderful purpose is to be able at the end of the process to present your vineyard to your lover in full bloom, so that you can both enjoy its fruit without regret or remorse. The intensity *of the waiting makes the final consummation all the more glorious. Failure should not lead us simply to guilt but to repentance, while God-enabled purity should not result in pride but profound thankfulness to God for his grace that protected us against ourselves.*

Yet not every good farmer who tends his vineyard carefully will enjoy the fruit of marriage. Some remain single for the long haul or struggle with same-sex attraction. Why continue to take good care of your vineyard when you don't see any way in which those blossoming vines will ever bear fruit in a biblically approved sexual relationship? Under those circumstances, watching and faithfully waiting easily seem like wasted labor.

Wait and Watch

There are two reasons still to wait and watch. The first reason is that God can surprise us with an unexpected relationship. People who have been single for many years may finally meet a godly spouse. Men and women whose struggle with same-sex attraction do in many cases get successfully married to a person of the opposite gender. Don't discount God's remarkable ability to confound your doom-and-gloom predictions for the future: He is the God who does far more than we can ask or imagine.

The second and far more important reason is that, whether or not we ever get married and find a beautiful and legitimate outlet for those God-given sexual desires, there is a greater lover for whom we are waiting. There is a God who desires you so passionately that he has moved heaven and earth to have a relationship with you. The powerful sexual drives God gives us to cement us together in marriage are only a pale reflection of how passionately God desires and pursues us.

Isaiah sang about his Beloved, who took perfect care of his vineyard (Isaiah 5). He dug it, cleared it of stones, and fertilized it; he built a wall around it and a watchtower to keep guard against foxes and other intruders. Yet when harvest time came, he found only a few sour and bitter grapes on the vines. Isaiah was describing God's love relationship with Israel, but he could just as easily have been describing the Lord's relationship with you and me.

The Lord has taken such good care of us and given us such abundant gifts — beauty, intellect, wealth, talent, opportunity, relationships, life itself — but the only fruit we have borne for him is wild and sour grapes. In our sexuality, he has given each of us a beautiful vineyard to watch over and we have razed down the wall, invited the foxes in for a party, planted thorns and thistles, and turned the whole thing into a muddy and sordid mess. Any normal landowner would call in the police to arrest such tenants.

But God is not any normal landowner. Instead, he sent his own Son to rescue and redeem his tenants from their own folly. Jesus came from the perfection of heaven and entered the muddy mess of this world in order to rebuild his vineyard. He came as a man with normal sexual appetites and desires that he knew he would not be able to fulfill. Yet he guarded his own vineyard perfectly, watching over it and waiting, not for the sake of a future earthly bride but for his heavenly bride, the church.

The bride that he chose has no beauty of her own and has not kept her own vineyard. She is dressed in the filthy rags of her abused sexuality, yet he came to clothe her in the beautiful garments of his own faithful watching and waiting so that, on her wedding day, she could be presented to him pure and spotless, beautiful beyond description. Jesus is the true Beloved for whom we are watching, the one for whom we are called to maintain our vineyards as we wait.

The ultimate harvest

So, we are not just to guard our vineyards for the sake of an earthly harvest, a wonderful vintage marriage to a good Christian man or woman. There is an ultimate harvest, a tree of life whose fruit we will taste on the last day when our waiting finally comes to an end with the return of the Bridegroom to claim his bride (Revelation 22:14). On that day, our cold and wandering hearts will finally be transformed and made whole. We shall behold the loveliness of his form with our own eyes. On that day, our joy will be complete as our Beloved says to us,

'Arise, my love, my beautiful one, and come away, for behold, the winter is past; the rain is over and gone. The flowers appear on the earth, the time of singing has come, and the voice of the turtledove is heard in our land. The fig tree ripens its figs, and the vines are in blossom; they give forth fragrance. Arise, my love, my beautiful one, and come away.' (Song of Solomon 2:10–13)

Copyright 2015 Iain Duguid. All rights reserved.

I love this article because it beautifully describes the process of waiting. However, we should not get so caught up in the waiting that it becomes our main focus. You then run the risk of missing out on the *now* by settling for less than the best in a rush to make the future happen sooner. This way you risk exchanging a life you will passionately embrace one day a time with a life where you simply exist as you look for the next part to come along. That's not what God wants for you!

Being single, just like being married, has a wonderful, God-given purpose that we should teach to our children. Far too many couples are married yet still feel lonely because they never fully understood what it meant to be fully single. Your future spouse deserves a completely whole, single person. You will know when you are completely content with your single status: When you *want* to be married one day, but don't *need* to be. Tony Evans, pastor and author, said, "Two good eggs joined together can make for a tasty omelet. Marriage can be wonderful, yes. But a single egg served over-easy, sunny side up or scrambled can be just as wonderful. Singleness affords you the unique opportunity to determine and discover what kind of eggs you truly enjoy most."

How to deal with questions about same sex relationships

By this age, your child might have a lot of questions with regard to same-sex relationships. As Christian parents, we cannot afford to have no opinion or to have a judgmental one. But how should we as Christian parents deal with it? There is so much confusion out there and the enemy loves confusion. He rolls in it like a pig in mud. The more confused we are, the more we can be deceived. But if we know what God says, we are like a house built on a rock. That is why we have to make sure we not only know what the Bible says, in context, but that we also know how to actively practice it the way Jesus did.

The enemy distorts sexuality in so many ways. Why? He wants to break up and destroy families, because he knows God's heart is all about families. The enemy hates God and, thus, he hates families. God's Word hasn't changed. People, culture, trends, and the modern world change all the time. What was *so* wrong yesterday is *so* accepted today. That is the first reason why we have to address the topic of same-sex relationships.

The second reason is because even though the majority of Christians are heterosexual (straight), there are some Christian teenagers and young adults who are attracted to people of the same sex. These young people might be judged, ridiculed and rejected by friends, family, and sadly, even some churches. It must be an excruciatingly painful experience to live through if people constantly throw mud at you, or if you are living a secret life, afraid of sharing your struggle. Others might embrace the gay lifestyle and accept it in all its forms, just as so many schools, governments and countries have. Gay marriage is legal in many countries, and those opposing it are often shamed and branded as homophobic and non-inclusive. Whatever your viewpoint, we are going to look at how we can talk about it with our children and deal with it if we are confronted with it.

So where do we start?

First of all, God loves you regardless of the sexual feelings you have. Yet how do we make sense of all this? And what do we teach our children? Stan Jones, a professor of psychology and a recognized Christian expert on sexuality, wrote an excellent book, *Homosexuality,* where he gives wonderful insight into this tricky part of sexuality.

There are a few Bible verses that some dedicated religious people use as weapons to back their viewpoints. These infamous Scriptures definitely made headlines in many church newsletters! However, they have been misquoted many times and should not be used as weapons, but rather as lessons.

These verses (Leviticus 18:22, 1 Corinthians 6:9-11, Romans 1:26–27) definitely state that God says that sexual intercourse between people of the same sex is wrong[26]. We can't cut it out and pretend God does not have an opinion about it. But in the same breath, God is also not happy with pride, adultery, unfaithfulness, sexual immorality and lying. These are all sins that straight people commit as well[26]. We all need God's grace and forgiveness! And guess what? Corinthians tells us that even if we do those things, we will be forgiven if we repent[26]. So, there's that.

But note that God *does not* say that he hates homosexuals, or that any other person has the right to hate them, judge them and treat them badly. God also does not say that homosexuality is unforgivable. Another thing that He doesn't say is that having feelings of attraction to a member of the same sex is sinful. (What?! … and you call yourself a Christian.) Remember, a desire to do what is sinful, is not wrong in itself. To want to have sex with someone you are attracted to is as natural as craving cake when you are on a diet. The sin comes in when you either go out and do it or take the steps to make it happen[26].

Our example will always be Jesus. He loves the sinner but not the sin. He calls us to leave our sinful lives and follow Him (John 8:11)[26]. He went beyond adultery to condemn even lust, even if the lust is only in our thoughts

(Matthew 5:27–30). Jesus died for all sinners, me and you included. He is not going to treat the homosexual any different from the one that told a lie, committed adultery, or gossiped. Treating others with love and kindness, no matter their beliefs, culture, race, sin, religion, or taste in eggs, is what our Father requires of us.

But somehow, we got a bit confused with all the so-called 'facts' out there. There are a few reasons for this confusion under Christians.

1. To be gay is quite common these days and this fact has led many to perceive being gay as normal and natural.

2. There is a firm belief in the world that gay people are born that way[26]. But the truth is that the cause is still a mystery. Science cannot prove it[24]. There is, however, something we all are born with, and that is a sinful nature. Blame the Edens… Adam and Eve Eden. Since sin entered the world, because of the Edens', we are all influenced by desires and brokenness we did not choose. The consequence of this is that some of us are born with inclinations or can easily develop inclinations towards things like drugs and alcohol, for example. Some give in to it, others choose not to. Sin is the cause, not God. Even those born without these inclinations make wrong choices anyway. We are all accountable for our choices, not our inclinations[26].

3. Another belief is that sexual orientation cannot be changed[26]. There are many testimonies of people all over the world that prove otherwise, even though the percentage is small[25]. A while ago I listened to a broadcast on the Focus on the Family website about a woman who beautifully describes her transformation and her conversion from being lesbian to being straight. There is so much hope, people! (If you want more understanding about how to be free from homosexuality, please listen to this broadcast on the *Focus on the Family* website, *Homosexuality and the 21st century church*. You can also visit www.restoredhopenetwork.org for more information.)

She explained that many people believe they are born gay or that God made them gay. If that is the case, then surely it must be okay to live the gay lifestyle and actively pursue it. But science cannot prove that it is genetic, in fact, never ever has it been found that there is a gene for homosexuality. And God is against it. God doesn't change, we do. God did not lower His standards, we lowered ours. God forbade Adam and Eve to eat from one specific tree. If we hang around that tree, look at it all the time, smell it, touch it, spend time with it, climb it and sit in its shade, it will not be long before we bite into the fruit. God has called us for so much more! He is calling us to the tree of Life. He is not calling us to hang around what is prohibited; He has called us to the fullness of life, Jesus, instead! God is not a mean guy! He did not make you to struggle with feelings of homosexuality and then prohibit you from acting on it. That doesn't make any sense. That is not who God is! God is in the business of transformation, to make you and your kids more and more like Jesus. God made our sexuality beautiful and to be enjoyed thoroughly and with passion—within His boundaries.

4. Another confusing matter is that young people sometimes experiment with such behavior, which confuses them even more. (Pornography has a massive influence on this.) What makes this even worse is that some even go through normal growing-up periods where their sexual feelings get a bit mixed up. If your child does have constant and strong feelings towards people of the same sex, please encourage them to talk about it with someone they trust. But I do urge you to carry on loving and accepting them and reminding them to choose God's life-giving way.

My question to you is this: Does living a homosexual lifestyle honor God, the Maker of families and marriages? Is that His original plan for us? He says that we were made in His image—male and female, He says that we must be fruitful and multiply, He says a man shall leave his parents and become one with his wife, God made Adam and Eve, He is rejoicing over us like a

Bridegroom over His bride, the whole book of Songs of Songs is a celebration of sexual love between a man and a woman. Our sexuality is a gift only to be practiced between a married man and his wife. Anything else is regarded as immoral by God. God is the One that thought of marriage. It was His idea! We have no right to change the dynamics of it. He has the copyright. Different cultures might color it in in different ways, but we are not allowed to change its foundational principles and original design. If we are trying to find our sexual identity anywhere else apart from Christ, we are heading for trouble. Your identity should not lie in your sexuality, no matter your sexual orientation. If it does, you will always take it personally and feel rejected for who you are as a person when the person of your affection rejects you or someone disagrees with your view. Yes, our sexuality is part of us, but it should not define us.

And for anyone who is attracted to the opposite sex and those of us who love people that are: sexuality is complicated. Don't condemn and judge people who believe differently and live differently from you. We live in a time when many gay and lesbian people are fighting for complete acceptance. Can we try to find the balance in showing them the love and acceptance of Jesus while also telling them the truth in love? We have all messed up in that department. We all sometimes lack the courage to tell the truth in love. Yet people who have different experiences deserve nothing less.

We cannot sweep homosexuality under the carpet because: 1) "God doesn't like it, so I don't like it—end of story", or 2) we are not comfortable to talk about it to our kids for whatever reason, or 3) we are scared that whoever doesn't agree with us is going to oppose us. They will oppose you. They will get defensive because truth sounds like hate to those who hate truth. And that is why you and your children need to know *why* you believe what you believe and *how* to get your viewpoint across if needed, in a respectful, kind-hearted, and loving way. We are not holier than anyone else just because we are straight. Loving God and loving our neighbors as ourselves are God's biggest commandments. Jesus does not say, "Love your neighbor as yourself when they believe what you believe and look like you and also have the same bank balance and live on the right side of the train tracks." No. Jesus says, "The second is this: 'Love your neighbor as yourself.' There is no commandment greater than these" (Mark 12:31). He included everyone in that Scripture. EVERYONE. And to really love someone, you need to know them. So, get to know your homosexual neighbor. Choose to love your homosexual neighbor and treat him or her with the same kindness and respect you want to be treated with. Only through our loving actions might our gay neighbors get to know Christ, not through judgmental words and body language. Only through our loving actions can we show acceptance for him or her as a person. And only through our own loving actions toward others, no matter who they are, will our children learn how to treat people who are different from them.

Afterthoughts

Including homosexuality in my book was a difficult choice. I rewrote this section several times. It changed from one short paragraph to many pages, back to only a few pages, and so forth. I was scared to 'offend'; I was scared to say too little or too much. In the end, after prayerfully working through each sentence, sharing it with people close to me, people not so close to me, parenting experts, and even gay people that I love and trust, I decided to stick to what you have just read. I decided to include this section because first and foremost, I believe every word in the Bible, and I will always try to say what He is saying. And secondly, so many parents have asked me, "Do you talk about homosexuality in your book? I have no idea how to approach this with my child." It is a genuine issue and Christian parents want answers.

Through this whole process of writing and rewriting this specific section, I also learned a few interesting facts about myself... I learned that no matter how hard I try, I cannot please everyone. Some will be offended, others will disagree, while others will agree. I decided to go with what I believe God is saying, no matter what.

I also learned that no matter how 'right' I think am, sometimes (well... many times), I am actually just plain self-righteous. Being sure of one's own biblical beliefs which are backed up by Scripture does not necessarily make one a kind, considerate, and loving human being. I saw that sometimes I sound exactly like the Pharisees and Sadducees who Jesus regularly had to... give a talking to, and a big heart-to-heart was needed—a few times—between me and God.

In saying that, it doesn't mean you should water down what you believe just because you are scared to offend, but rather say what you believe with love and consideration. Always speak God's truth, the *way* Jesus did, but also *like* Jesus did... Sometimes we forget that part. Jesus showed us clearly how to deal with humans, sinful or not. His words were action ALL THE TIME. His love was action ALL THE TIME. And his earthly example is what we should strive to follow ALL THE TIME.

A concerned parent (me): "But what about the boy in my child's class with two moms? Or the gay student that started the new school year? Or the transgender girl in my child's class? How do I explain that to my child? What do I say?".

In the end, it boils down to something as simple as the following:

Me: "Remember the 7 P's as practiced in *Chapter 5*".

Peter: "But in your hearts revere Christ as Lord. Always be prepared to give an answer to everyone who asks you to give the reason for the hope that you have. But do this with gentleness and respect". (1 Peter 3:15)

Jesus: "Love your neighbor as yourself". (Matthew 22:39, Mark 12:31, James 2:8, Galatians 5:14)

LET'S GET PRACTICAL

STUFF TO DO:

- Draw two triangles or find other objects that can visually assist you in your discussion about Hollywood's ideas of relationships versus God's ideas of relationships.
- Make a list of all the people you and your spouse have dated and write down the physical, emotional, mental, social, and spiritual consequences you have experienced.
- Take the abovementioned information and work through it systematically with your teenager, discussing each point and, if necessary, doing more research, explaining *why* it is important to know about the consequences of our sexual choices.
- Do an honest heart-check about how you act when it comes to people who are different from you, who believe differently and who act differently—even if you consider their behavior as sinful. Take your heart to God and let Him rectify any wrong mindsets you might have. Meditate on Matthew 22:39.

STUFF TO TALK ABOUT:

- Discuss these triangles with your children, as well as the consequences you and your spouse have suffered due to being in previous serious relationships or living with a romantic partner. The reason that it is so important to discuss these effects and consequences on a regular basis is because the teenage brain is not yet fully developed, and their ability to consider long-term consequences, the bigger picture and future outcomes is not properly in place yet. Your experiences (or those of others who have experienced these consequences) can serve as a lesson or a tool for them to assist them in their choices.

- Explain to your children why waiting for marriage to have sex is important.
- Talk about the purpose of being single.
- Also discuss the reasons why Christians believe that homosexuality is not part of God's will. In the same breath, discuss ways in which you as a family can still show love and kindness to gay people. Teach your children why it is important to God that we love our neighbors, even if they are different from us. Teach them Matthew 22:39, and then be an example.

RECOMMENDED RESOURCES:

- *God is a Matchmaker*, by Derek and Ruth Prince
- *When God Writes Your Love Story*, by Eric and Leslie Ludy
- *Kingdom Marriage*, by Tony Evans
- *Facing the Facts*, by Stan and Brenna Jones
- *Homosexuality*, by Stan Jones

SCRIPTURES:

Genesis 24 *[Please refer to the whole of Genesis 24 for the story of Isaac and Rebekah.]*

Song of Solomon 2:7 Daughters of Jerusalem, I charge you by the gazelles and by the does of the field: Do not arouse or awaken love until it so desires.

John 8:11 "No one, sir," she said.
"Then neither do I condemn you," Jesus declared. "Go now and leave your life of sin."

John 16:33 "I have told you these things, so that in me you may have peace. In this world you will have trouble. But take heart! I have overcome the world."

Galatians 6:9 Let us not become weary in doing good, for at the proper time we will reap a harvest if we do not give up.

Matthew 5:27–30 You have heard that it was said, "You shall not commit adultery." But I tell you that anyone who looks at a woman lustfully has already committed adultery with her in his heart. If your right eye causes you to stumble, gouge it out and throw it away. It is better for you to lose one part of your body than for your whole body to be thrown into hell. And if your right hand causes you to stumble, cut it off and throw it away. It is better for you to lose one part of your body than for your whole body to go into hell.

Matthew 22:39 And the second is like it: "Love your neighbor as yourself."

Mark 12:31 The second is this: 'Love your neighbor as yourself.' There is no commandment greater than these.

Galatians 5:14 For the entire law is fulfilled in keeping this one command: "Love your neighbor as yourself."

James 2:8 If you really keep the royal law found in Scripture, "Love your neighbor as yourself," you are doing right.

1 Peter 3:15 But in your hearts revere Christ as Lord. Always be prepared to give an answer to everyone who asks you to give the reason for the hope that you have. But do this with gentleness and respect.

CHAPTER 11

TEACH THEM TO BE REAL... IN FRONT OF GOD

Sometimes our past choices can keep us from sharing openly with our children about sex. Is that the case for you? Have you messed up? Do you carry baggage and condemnation because of your sexual past? Were you raised in a legalistic home with unhealthy religious views about sex?

Asking God's forgiveness—forgiving yourself and others who have hurt or abused you sexually (or in other ways)—is possible. Just do it. Asking God to set you free and deliver you from wrong viewpoints, fear and legalistic religious nonsense is also possible. If you have any struggles in this area, please get help for it. There are many people who are trained and willing to help you through the process of healing and forgiveness. Ask God to renew your mind and your heart. Do not believe the lie that nobody cares, because that is not true. Open the floodgates so that your healing can start. Open the can so that the worms can come out. Take off the scab so that the icky yellow stuff can come out. A broken parent can't help a broken child. We repeat what we don't repair, and what you allow is what will continue. The better you deal with life and the better you deal with your issues, mistakes and hurt, the better it is for everyone in your household and the better you can teach that to your children. Truth is like surgery: it hurts, but it cures. Lies are like painkillers: it provides some relief but has lasting side effects. It's up to us to choose whether we are going to carry on believing lies or not. I once read somewhere that if we don't heal from that which hurt us, we bleed on people who didn't cut us. Those are very true words!

The consequences of your past mistakes, choices or sins might still be present in your life. Sexual memories and hurts from the past can still linger. The pregnant girl from long ago can still be plagued by memories of and guilt over things passed and thoughts of the child she gave up. You might still be infertile, or you might still have the STD. You might still suffer from depression, be in a wheelchair or drink too much. You might still be in jail or be divorced, in therapy or learning to deal with a broken relationship. You might still suffer from guilt, shame or pain.

Whatever the consequences you are dealing with, God's forgiveness has a way of healing in such a complete way that our past sins do not immobilize us anymore. He loves you more than you can imagine. He is your Father, which makes you His child. He will do anything for you—He gave His LIFE for you. Take that gift of life and make it yours!

Another important factor to consider is to keep in mind that your children might have already made unhealthy sexual choices or have struggles with purity of mind and heart. Ask the Lord to show you the struggles your children face and how to deal with it. Let's show them how to be real before God and how to bring even our darkest secrets to Him. Teach them to do the same: *Confess, repent, and ask God to restore what was lost or broken.*

Enough of pretending to be the perfect parent, to have the perfect child or even the perfect 'not-so-perfect'. Salvador Dali once famously said, "Have no fear of perfection; you will never reach it."
Enough of pride, justification and 'my oh-so-valid reasoning'.

Enough of self-pity, past mistakes, fears, and the blaming of others. Enough of letting others do the work, teach the concepts, and take the responsibility. Save the excuses—it's not about *having* time; it's about *making* time. If it matters, you will make time.

Here is some tough-love medicine to chew on… You need to get over it if you messed up—in your own life and in your parenting. Enter His courtroom, fight it out, be real, open, and honest before God, and let it all out. Repent, take responsibility, accept His forgiveness, make the most of the consequences and move on. Stop lingering in shame and guilt, because it is only then that you will be able to walk in freedom and teach your children to do the same.

Our most precious gift of sexuality is meant to be protected and it is there to be enjoyed thoroughly with your spouse. Deal with your past so that you can indulge with no shame, fear, or regrets. Let's teach our children how to do it God's way, so that they can also freely enjoy a loving and passionate relationship with their spouses. It really is a gift available to everyone!

Hosea 2:18–19 I will make you my wife forever, showing you righteousness and justice, unfailing love, and compassion. I will be faithful to you and make you mine, and you will finally know me as the LORD.

When you read this Scripture now, after reading the whole book, doesn't it just make so much more sense? It even includes all 7 P's!

Look at God's promises in these verses:

- "I will make you my wife forever"—ultimate commitment
- "showing you righteousness and justice"—ultimate protection
- "unfailing love and compassion"—unconditional love, care and understanding that never stops and never will stop

- "I will be faithful and make you mine"—He will never leave you, you are His forever
- "and you will finally know me as the LORD"—ultimate intimacy (in-to-me-you-see) because you will *know* Him

My prayer for you is that you and your children will fully experience this passionate and zealous declaration from God and that it will manifest itself in your life, your marriage, and the marriages of your children!

LET'S GET PRACTICAL

STUFF TO DO:

- First, take your own sin and pain to God. We all have to do that. Lay it at His feet and ask the Holy Spirit to show you if there is anything in your heart that is not from Him. Ask Him to show you any 'heart splinter' that you need to deal with.
- Show your children how to do the same. Teaching them to repent is a process that will take time.
- Show your children real life. Take them to an AA meeting, rehabilitation center, orphanage, house for pregnant teenage girls, children's homes, safe houses, or any like places in your community. It will show them:
  1. the consequences of unhealthy choices, by themselves or by others.
  2. that help is available.
  3. God's grace. When you volunteer at these centers you will see how God is working.

STUFF TO TALK ABOUT:

- If you are comfortable in sharing your past mistakes with your teenager, then please do so. They need to see that their parents are also human. It will make them more willing to approach you with their own struggles and sin.

- Talk about past and present hurts.
- Pray Proverbs 2:6 together: "Father, give my child wisdom."

RECOMMENDED RESOURCES:

- *Sex in a Broken World: How Christ Redeems What Sin Distorts*, by Paul David Tripp
- *Heart Splinters*, by Lisa Max

SCRIPTURES:

Psalm 86:5 You, Lord, are forgiving and good, abounding in love to all who call to you.

Mark 11:25 And when you stand praying, if you hold anything against anyone, forgive them, so that your Father in heaven may forgive you your sins.

Hebrews 8:12 For I will forgive their wickedness and will remember their sins no more.

Daniel 9:9 The Lord our God is merciful and forgiving, even though we have rebelled against him.

Psalm 139:24 See if there is any offensive way in me, and lead me in the way everlasting.

Proverbs 2:6 For the Lord gives wisdom; from his mouth come knowledge and understanding.

GET IN TOUCH

Enjoy this book? You can make a big difference!

Reviews are one of the most powerful tools in my arsenal when it comes to spreading God's plan for our sexuality all over the world. Honest reviews of this book will help bring it to the attention of other parents. In this way we all contribute to assist Christian parents in parenting sexuality—God's way!

If you found this book helpful, I would be very grateful if you could spend just five minutes leaving a review (it can be as short as you like) on the book's retailers' page.

Thank you very much.

Social Media

If you would like to connect with me and our community of parents, you can:

- Join my mailing list at www.zaleadold.com

- Send me an email at info@zaleadold.com

- Follow me on:

  facebook.com/theBirdstheBeesandtheBible

  @thebirdsthebeesandthebible

REFERENCES

1. Chandra, A., Mosher, W.D., Copen, C. & Sionean, C. 2011. Sexual behavior, sexual attraction, and sexual identity in the United States. *National Health Statistics Reports* 36. Online Report. Accessed from http://www.cdc.gov.

2. Kann, L. 2016. Youth risk behavior surveillance—United States, 2015. *Surveillance Summaries* 65(6). Online Report. Accessed from https://www.cdc.gov.

3. Kost, K. & Maddow-Zimet, I. 2016. U.S. teenage pregnancies, births and abortions, 2011: National trends by age, race and ethnicity. Online Report. Accessed from https://www.guttmacher.org.

4. Martinez, G., Copen, C.E. & Abma, J.C. 2011. Teenagers in the United States: Sexual activity, contraceptive use, and childbearing, 2006-2010 National Survey of Family Growth. *Vital Health Statistics* 23(31). Online Report. Accessed from http://www.cdc.gov.

5. Kann, L., Kinchen, S., Shanklin, S.L., Flint, K.H., Hawkins, J., Harris, W.A. & Zaza, S. 2014. Youth risk behavior surveillance—United States, 2013. *Surveillance Summaries* 63(4). Accessed from http://www.cdc.gov.

6. Manlove, J., Ryan, S. & Franzetta, K. 2004. Contraceptive use and consistency in U.S. teenagers' most recent sexual relationships. *Perspectives on Sexual & Reproductive Health* 36(6): 265-275. Online Journal. Accessed from https://www.guttmacher.org.

7. The 2019 year in review. 2019. Online review. Accessed from https://www.pornhub.com/insights.

8. Aaron, C. 2018. 4,000% Explosion in Kids Identifying as Transgender, Docs Perform Double Mastectomies on Healthy Teen Girls. Online article. Accessed from www1.cbn.com.

9. Showalter, B. 2020. 1,500% increase in teen girls diagnosed with gender dysphoria in Sweden. Online article. Accessed from www.christiantoday.com.

10. Finer, L.B. & Zolna, M.R. 2016. Declines in Unintended Pregnancy in the United States, 2008–2011. *New England Journal of Medicine* 374(9):843–852. Online Journal. Accessed from http://nejm.org.

11. 2020. Online Article. Accessed from https://www.healthypeople.gov/2020/topics-objectives/topic/sexually-transmitted-diseases.

12. Online Article. Accessed from https://www.Change.org.

13. Diamant, J. 2020. Half of US Christians say Casual Sex between Consenting Adults is Sometimes or Always Acceptable. Online Article. Accessed from https://www.pewresearch.org.

14. Slattery, J. 2018. Promise rings and Purity Talks Aren't Enough. Online article. Accessed from www.boundless.org.

15. Slattery, J. 2020. What is the purpose of sexuality if I am single? Online article. Accessed from www.boundless.org.

16. Lee, N. & Lee, S. 2011. *The Parenting Children Course.* London: Alpha International.

17. Meeker, M. 2007. *Your kids at risk: How teen sex threatens our sons and daughters.* Washington, D.C: Regnery Publishing.

18. Tverberg, L. 2015. Ish & Ishah – Together Fully Human. Online Article. Accessed from www.engediresourcecenter.com.

19. Tankard Reist, M. 2018. Sex before kissing: How 15-year-old girls are dealing with porn addicted boys. Online Article. Accessed from www.tosavealife.com.

20. McNamara, H. 2018. Three Ways Domestic Violence is Connected to Pornography. Online Article. Accessed from www.endsexualexploitation.org.

21. Dr. Darleen Edwards-Meyer. Accessed from www.drdarleen.co.za.

22. LaMotte, S. 2020. Are you in love or just high on chemicals in your brain? Answer: Yes. Online Article. Accessed from https://edition.cnn.com.

23. Duguid, I. 2015. Waiting to Awaken Love. Online Article. Accessed from https://www.desiringgod.org.

24. Långström, N., Rahman, Q., Carlström, E., *et al* 2010. Genetic and Environmental Effects on Same-sex Sexual Behavior: A Population Study of Twins in Sweden. *Arch Sex Behav* 39(1): 75–80. Online Report. Accessed from https://doi.org.

25. Jones, S. & Yarhouse, M. 2007. *Ex-Gays?: An Extended Longitudinal Study of Attempted Religiously Mediated Change in Sexual Orientation.* Downers Grove, Illinois: InterVarsity Press.

26. Jones, S. & Jones, B. 2019. *Facing the Facts: The Truth About Sex & You.* Third edition. Carol Stream, Illinois: NavPress.

27. Palmer, S. 2015. *Toxic Childhood.* Updated paperback edition. London: Orion Books Ltd.

28. Max, L. 2021. *THIS IS WAR - Day One - 2/3 – CAUGHT WITH YOUR HANDS IN THE COOKIE JAR.* [Facebook]. 10 August 2020. [Accessed 16 March 2021]. Accessed from

https://www.facebook.com/groups/Letthechildrenfly/permalink/27462
45448985410.

29. Jones, S. & Jones, B. 2007. *How and When to Tell Your Kids About Sex.*
Second edition. Colorado Springs, Colorado: NavPress.

The author gratefully acknowledges permission to reproduce copyright material in this book. Every effort has been made to retrieve permission from all copyright holders. If there are any unintended omissions, the author apologizes to the concerned parties and will ensure that necessary acknowledgments are made in all future editions.

ABOUT THE AUTHOR

Teaching art and design has always been my thing. Teaching sexuality, however, has always been my passion. After completing my degree in Education, I taught high school students, youth groups and parents for almost 20 years, and worked with many professionals in Sexuality Education.

My family and I immigrated from South Africa to the Netherlands in 2018, and the first year was consumed by immigration administration and trying to find our feet in a new country with a language we couldn't speak. I had quit my day job as a teacher in South Africa to become a full-time housewife in the Netherlands—one with hundreds of open tabs and no idea where the music is coming from! Add to the mix a whole lot of language lessons, bipolar emotional rides, and a serious lack of Dutch cycling skills, and you get a pretty tough 2019… Your typical 2020, mind you. The Covid-19 lockdown came as a blessing in disguise: I went from balancing an ironing board, a child and a printer on a bicycle with two shopping bags dangling from the handlebar (all at the same time) to a time and space to finally find my words. I started expressing myself through writing and taking painting classes over Zoom—I hadn't painted for years, out of fear for not being good enough. I discovered two things: My writing makes people laugh and cry at the same time, much like my cycling, and I absolutely love painting with words as much as with oils. I started writing my first book, *The Birds, the Bees & the Bible—How to Practically Parent Sexuality*, because God said that it was time and that He has something to say that people need to hear, and I just couldn't keep all the words inside anymore. My life took a major turn after our immigration… and I loved it!

But there is more to my story: I was super shy for much of my life and had no idea how to express myself. I tried to join the debate team at age 12 and failed miserably. I also tried to join a public speaking contest at school, but not only did I choose a topic that no-one found amusing, but also hit a blank after the first two sentences and went back to my seat red-faced and humiliated, vowing to never ever voice my opinion on anything ever again. I received the lowest score and the most pitiful looks that day.

It was a long road from fear and silence into joy and freedom of expression. Yet this is what makes my writing meaningful to me: I vividly remember what it's like to be shut down. But I also know the exhilaration and power of facing your fears, finding your words, and expressing your true self, no matter the medium and no matter what others might say.

Now it's time to walk in my purpose.

Made in the USA
Las Vegas, NV
08 May 2024

89666525R00135